Big Data: A Very Short Introduction

VERY SHORT INTRODUCTIONS are for anyone wanting a stimulating and accessible way into a new subject. They are written by experts, and have been translated into more than 45 different languages.

The series began in 1995, and now covers a wide variety of topics in every discipline. The VSI library now contains over 500 volumes—a Very Short Introduction to everything from Psychology and Philosophy of Science to American History and Relativity—and continues to grow in every subject area.

Very Short Introductions available now:

Available soon:

For more information visit our website

www.oup.com/vsi/

Dawn E. Holmes

BIG DATA

A Very Short Introduction

OXFORD
UNIVERSITY PRESS

OXFORD

UNIVERSITY PRESS

Great Clarendon Street, Oxford, OX2 6DP,
United Kingdom

Oxford University Press is a department of the University of Oxford.
It furthers the University's objective of excellence in research, scholarship,
and education by publishing worldwide. Oxford is a registered trade mark of
Oxford University Press in the UK and in certain other countries

© Dawn E. Holmes 2017

The moral rights of the author have been asserted

First edition published in 2017

Impression: 7

Published in the United States of America by Oxford University Press
198 Madison Avenue, New York, NY 10016, United States of America

British Library Cataloguing in Publication Data
Data available

Library of Congress Control Number: 2017942731

ISBN 978-0-19-877957-5

Printed and bound by CPI Group (UK) Ltd, Croydon, CR0 4YY

Links to third party websites are provided by Oxford in good faith and
for information only. Oxford disclaims any responsibility for the materials
contained in any third party website referenced in this work.

Contents

Preface

Books on big data tend to fall into one of two categories: either they offer no explanation as to how things actually work or they are highly mathematical textbooks suitable only for graduate students. The aim of this book is to offer an alternative by providing an introduction to how big data works and is changing the world about us; the effect it has on our everyday lives; and the effect it has in the business world.

Data used to mean documents and papers, with maybe a few photos, but it now means much more than that. Social networking sites generate large amounts of data in the form of images, videos, and movies on a minute by minute basis. Online shopping creates data as we enter our address and credit card details. We are now at a point where the collection and storage of data is growing at a rate unimaginable only a few decades ago but, as we will see in this book, new data analysis techniques are transforming this data into useful information. While writing this book, I found that big data cannot be meaningfully discussed without frequent reference to its collection, storage, analysis, and use by the big commercial players. Since research departments in companies such as Google and Amazon have been responsible for many of the major developments in big data, frequent reference will be made to them.

The first chapter introduces the reader to the diversity of data in general before explaining how the digital age has led to changes in the way we define data. Big data is introduced informally through the idea of the data explosion, which involves computer science, statistics, and the interface between them. In Chapters 2 to 4, I have used diagrams quite extensively to help explain some of the new methods required by big data. The second chapter explores what makes big data special and, in doing so, leads us to a more specific definition. In Chapter 3, we discuss the problems related to storing and managing big data. Most people are familiar with the need to back up the data on their personal computer. But how do we do this with the colossal amounts of data that are now being generated? To answer this question, we will look at database storage and the idea of distributing tasks across clusters of computers. Chapter 4 argues that big data is only useful if we can extract useful information from it. A flavour of how data is turned into information is given using simplified explanations of several well-established techniques.

We then move on to a more detailed discussion of big data applications, starting in Chapter 5 with the role of big data in medicine. Chapter 6 analyses business practices with case studies on Amazon and Netflix, each highlighting different features of marketing using big data. Chapter 7 looks at some of the security issues surrounding big data and the importance of encryption. Data theft has become a big problem and we look at some of the cases that have been in the news including Snowden and WikiLeaks. The chapter concludes by showing how cybercrime is an issue that big data needs to address. In the final chapter, Chapter 8, we consider how big data is changing the society we live in, through the development of sophisticated robots and their role in the workplace. A consideration of the smart homes and smart cities of the future concludes the book.

In a very short introduction it is not possible to mention everything, so I hope the reader will pursue their interests through the Further reading section's recommendations.

Acknowledgements

When I mentioned to Peter that I wanted to acknowledge his contribution to this book, he suggested the following: 'I would like to thank Peter Harper, without whose dedicated use of the spell-checker this would have been a different book.' I would also thank him for his expertise in coffee-making and his sense of humour! By itself, this support is invaluable but Peter did much, much more and it is true to say that without his unwavering encouragement and constructive contributions, this book would not have been written.

Dawn E. Holmes

April 2017

List of illustrations

Chapter 1
The data explosion

What is data?

In 431 BCE, Sparta declared war on Athens. Thucydides, in his account of the war, describes how besieged Plataean forces loyal to Athens planned to escape by scaling the wall surrounding Plataea built by Spartan-led Peloponnesian forces. To do this they needed to know how high the wall was so that they could make ladders of suitable length. Much of the Peloponnesian wall had been covered with rough pebbledash, but a section was found where the bricks were still clearly visible and a large number of soldiers were each given the task of counting the layers of these exposed bricks. Working at a distance safe from enemy attack inevitably introduced mistakes, but as Thucydides explains, given that many counts were taken, the result that appeared most often would be correct. This most frequently occurring count, which we would now refer to as *the mode*, was then used to calculate the height of the wall, the Plataeans knowing the size of the local bricks used, and ladders of the length required to scale the wall were constructed. This enabled a force of several hundred men to escape, and the episode may well be considered the most impressive example of historic data collection and analysis. But the collection, storage, and analysis of data pre-dates even Thucydides by many centuries, as we will see.

Notches have been found on sticks, stones, and bones dating back to as early as the Upper Paleolithic era. These notches are thought to represent data stored as tally marks, though this is still open to academic debate. Perhaps the most famous example is the Ishango Bone, found in the Democratic Republic of Congo in 1950, and which is estimated to be around 20,000 years old. This notched bone has been variously interpreted as a calculator or a calendar, although others prefer to explain the notches as being there just to provide a better grip. The Lebombo Bone, discovered in the 1970s in Swaziland, is even older, dating from around 35,000 BCE. With twenty-nine lines scored across it, this fragment of a baboon's fibula bears a striking resemblance to the calendar sticks still used by bushmen in distant Namibia, suggesting that this may indeed be a method that was used to keep track of data important to their civilization.

While the interpretation of these notched bones is still open to speculation, we know that one of the first well-documented uses of data is the census undertaken by the Babylonians in 3800 BCE. This census systematically documented population numbers and commodities, such as milk and honey, in order to provide the information necessary to calculate taxes. The early Egyptians also used data, in the form of hieroglyphs written on wood or papyrus, to record the delivery of goods and to keep track of taxes. But early examples of data usage are by no means confined to Europe and Africa. The Incas and their South American predecessors, keen to record statistics for tax and commercial purposes, used a sophisticated and complex system of coloured knotted strings, called *quipu*, as a decimal-based accounting system. These knotted strings, made from brightly dyed cotton or camelid wool, date back to the third millennium BCE, and although fewer than a thousand are known to have survived the Spanish invasion and subsequent attempt to eradicate them, they are among the first known examples of a massive data storage system. Computer algorithms are now being developed to try to decode the full meaning of the *quipu* and enhance our understanding of how they were used.

Although we can think of and describe these early systems as using data, the word 'data' is actually a plural word of Latin origin, with 'datum' being the singular. 'Datum' is rarely used today and 'data' is used for both singular and plural. The *Oxford English Dictionary* attributes the first known use of the term to the 17th-century English cleric Henry Hammond in a controversial religious tract published in 1648. In it Hammond used the phrase 'heap of data', in a theological sense, to refer to incontrovertible religious truths. But although this publication stands out as representing the first use of the term 'data' in English, it does not capture its use in the modern sense of denoting facts and figures about a population of interest. 'Data', as we now understand the term, owes its origins to the scientific revolution in the 18th century led by intellectual giants such as Priestley, Newton, and Lavoisier; and, by 1809, following the work of earlier mathematicians, Gauss and Laplace were laying the highly mathematical foundations for modern statistical methodology.

On a more practical level, an extensive amount of data was collected on the 1854 cholera outbreak in Broad Street, London, allowing physician John Snow to chart the outbreak. By doing so, he was able to lend support to his hypothesis that contaminated water spread the disease and to show that it was not airborne as had been previously believed. Gathering data from local inhabitants he established that those affected were all using the same public water pump; he then persuaded the local parish authorities to shut it down, a task they accomplished by removing the pump handle. Snow subsequently produced a map, now famous, showing that the illness had occurred in clusters around the Broad Street pump. He continued to work in this field, collecting and analysing data, and is renowned as a pioneering epidemiologist.

Following John Snow's work, epidemiologists and social scientists have increasingly found demographic data invaluable for research purposes, and the census now taken in many countries proves a useful source of such information. For example, data on the birth and death rate, the frequency of various diseases, and statistics on income and crime is all now collected, which was not the case prior to the 19th century. The census, which takes place every ten years in most countries, has been collecting increasing amounts of data, which eventually has resulted in more than could realistically be recorded by hand or the simple tallying machines previously used. The challenge of processing these ever-increasing amounts of census data was in part met by Herman Hollerith while working for the US Census Bureau.

By the 1870 US census, a simple tallying machine was in operation but this had limited success in reducing the work of the Census Bureau. A breakthrough came in time for the 1890 census, when Herman Hollerith's punched cards tabulator for storing and processing data was used. The time taken to process the US census data was usually about eight years, but using this new invention the time was reduced to one year. Hollerith's machine revolutionized the analysis of census data in countries worldwide, including Germany, Russia, Norway, and Cuba.

Hollerith subsequently sold his machine to the company that evolved into IBM, which then developed and produced a widely used series of punch card machines. In 1969, the American National Standards Institute (ANSI) defined the Hollerith Punched Card Code (or Hollerith Card Code), honouring Hollerith for his early punch card innovations.

Data in the digital age

Before the widespread use of computers, data from the census, scientific experiments, or carefully designed sample surveys and questionnaires was recorded on paper—a process that was time-consuming and expensive. Data collection could only take place once researchers had decided which questions they wanted their experiments or surveys to answer, and the resulting highly structured data, transcribed onto paper in ordered rows and columns, was then amenable to traditional methods of statistical analysis. By the first half of the 20th century some data was being stored on computers, helping to alleviate some of this labour-intensive work, but it was through the launch of the World Wide Web (or Web) in 1989, and its rapid development, that it became increasingly feasible to generate, collect, store, and analyse data electronically. The problems inevitably generated by the very large volume of data made accessible by the Web then needed to be addressed, and we first look at how we may make distinctions between different types of data.

The data we derive from the Web can be classified as structured, unstructured, or semi-structured.

Structured data, of the kind written by hand and kept in notebooks or in filing cabinets, is now stored electronically on spreadsheets or databases, and consists of spreadsheet-style tables with rows and columns, each row being a record and each column a well-defined field (e.g. name, address, and age). We are contributing to these structured data stores when, for example, we provide the information necessary to order goods online. Carefully structured and tabulated data is relatively easy to manage and is amenable to statistical analysis, indeed until recently statistical analysis methods could be applied only to structured data.

In contrast, unstructured data is not so easily categorized and includes photos, videos, tweets, and word-processing documents. Once the use of the World Wide Web became widespread, it transpired that many such potential sources of information remained inaccessible because they lacked the structure needed for existing analytic techniques to be applied. However, by identifying key features, data that appears at first sight to be unstructured may not be completely without structure. Emails, for example, contain structured *metadata* in the heading as well as the actual unstructured message in the text and so may be classified as semi-structured data. Metadata tags, which are essentially descriptive references, can be used to add some structure to unstructured data. Adding a word tag to an image on a website makes it identifiable and so easier to search for. Semi-structured data is also found on social networking sites, which use hashtags so that messages (which are unstructured data) on a particular topic can be identified. Dealing with unstructured data is challenging: since it cannot be stored in traditional databases or spreadsheets, special tools have had to be developed to extract useful information. In later chapters we will look at how unstructured data is stored.

The term 'data explosion', which heads this chapter, refers to the increasingly vast amounts of structured, unstructured, and semi-structured data being generated minute by minute; we will look next at some of the many different sources that produce all this data.

Introduction to big data

Just in researching material for this book I have been swamped by the sheer volume of data available on the Web—from websites, scientific journals, and e-textbooks. According to a recent worldwide study conducted by IBM, about 2.5 *exabytes* (Eb) of data are generated every day. One Eb is 10^{18} (1 followed by eighteen 0s) bytes (or a million *terabytes* (Tb); see the Big data byte size chart at the end of this book). A good laptop bought at the time of writing will typically have a hard drive with 1 or 2 Tb of storage space. Originally, the term 'big data' simply referred to the very large amounts of data being produced in the digital age. These huge amounts of data, both structured and unstructured, include all the Web data generated by emails, websites, and social networking sites.

Approximately 80 per cent of the world's data is unstructured in the form of text, photos, and images, and so it is not amenable to the traditional methods of structured data analysis. 'Big data' is now used to refer not just to the total amount of data generated and stored electronically, but also to specific datasets that are large in both size and complexity, with which new algorithmic techniques are required in order to extract useful information from them. These big datasets come from different sources so let's take a more detailed look at some of them and the data they generate.

Search engine data

In 2015, Google was by far the most popular search engine worldwide, with Microsoft's Bing and Yahoo Search coming second and third, respectively. In 2012, the most recent year for which data is publicly available, there were over 3.5 billion searches made per day on Google alone.

Entering a key term into a search engine generates a list of the most relevant websites, but at the same time a considerable amount of data is being collected. Web tracking generates big data. As an exercise, I searched on 'border collies' and clicked on the top website returned. Using some basic tracking software, I found that some sixty-seven third-party site connections were generated just by clicking on this one website. In order to track the interests of people who access the site, information is being shared in this way between commercial enterprises.

Every time we use a search engine, logs are created recording which of the recommended sites we visited. These logs contain useful information such as the query term itself, the IP address of the device used, the time when the query was submitted, how long we stayed on each site, and in which order we visited them—all without identifying us by name. In addition, *clickstream logs* record the path taken as we visit various websites as well as our navigation within each website. When we surf the Web, every click we make is recorded somewhere for future use. Software is available for businesses allowing them to collect the clickstream data generated by their own website—a valuable marketing tool. For example, by providing data on the use of the system, logs can help detect malicious activity such as identity theft. Logs are also used to gauge the effectiveness of online advertising, essentially by counting the number of times an advertisement is clicked on by a website visitor.

By enabling customer identification, cookies are used to personalize your surfing experience. When you make your first visit to a chosen website, a *cookie*, which is a small text file, usually consisting of a website identifier and a user identifier, will be sent to your computer, unless you have blocked the use of cookies. Each time you visit this website, the cookie sends a message back to the website and in this way keeps track of your visits. As we will see in Chapter 6, cookies are often used to record clickstream data, to keep track of your preferences, or to add your name to targeted advertising.

Social networking sites also generate a vast amount of data, with Facebook and Twitter at the top of the list. By the middle of 2016, Facebook had, on average, 1.71 billion active users per month, all generating data, resulting in about 1.5 *petabytes* (Pb; or 1,000 Tb) of Web log data every day. YouTube, the popular video-sharing website, has had a huge impact since it started in 2005, and a recent YouTube press release claims that there are over a billion users worldwide. The valuable data produced by search engines and social networking sites can be used in many other areas, for example when dealing with health issues.

Healthcare data

If we look at healthcare we find an area which involves a large and growing percentage of the world population and which is increasingly computerized. Electronic health records are gradually becoming the norm in hospitals and doctors' surgeries, with the primary aim being to make it easier to share patient data with other hospitals and physicians, and so to facilitate the provision of better healthcare. The collection of personal data through wearable or implantable sensors is on the increase, particularly for health monitoring, with many of us using personal fitness trackers of varying complexity which output ever more categories of data. It is now possible to monitor a patient's health remotely in real-time through the collection of data on blood pressure, pulse, and temperature, thus potentially reducing healthcare costs and improving quality of life. These remote monitoring devices are becoming increasingly sophisticated and now go beyond basic measurements to include sleep tracking and arterial oxygen saturation rate.

Some companies offer incentives in order to persuade employees to use a wearable fitness device and to meet certain targets such as weight loss or a certain number of steps taken per day. In return for being given the device, the employee agrees to share the data with the employer. This may seem reasonable but there will inevitably be privacy issues to be considered, together with the unwelcome pressure some people may feel under to opt into such a scheme.

Other forms of employee monitoring are becoming more frequent, such as tracking all employee activities on the company-provided computers and smartphones. Using customized software, this tracking can include everything from monitoring which websites are visited to logging individual keystrokes and checking whether the computer is being used for private purposes such as visiting social network sites. In the age of massive data leaks, security is of growing concern and so corporate data must be protected. Monitoring emails and tracking websites visited are just two ways of reducing the theft of sensitive material.

As we have seen, personal health data may be derived from sensors, such as a fitness tracker or health monitoring device. However, much of the data being collected from sensors is for highly specialized medical purposes. Some of the largest data stores in existence are being generated as researchers study the genes and sequencing genomes of a variety of species. The structure of the deoxyribonucleic acid molecule (DNA), famous for holding the genetic instructions for the functioning of living organisms, was first described as a double-helix by James Watson and Francis Crick in 1953. One of the most highly publicized research projects in recent years has been the international human genome project, which determines the sequence, or exact order, of the three billion base-pairs that comprise human DNA. Ultimately, this data is helping research teams in the study of genetic diseases.

Real-time data

Some data is collected, processed, and used in real-time. The increase in computer processing power has allowed an increase in the ability to process as well as generate such data rapidly. These are systems where response time is crucial and so data must be processed in a timely manner. For example, the Global Positioning System (GPS) uses a system of satellites to scan the Earth and send back huge amounts of real-time data. A GPS receiving device, maybe in your car or smartphone ('smart' indicates that an item, in this case a phone, has Internet access and the ability to provide a number of services or applications (apps) that can then be linked together), processes these satellite signals and calculates your position, time, and speed.

This technology is now being used in the development of driverless or autonomous vehicles. These are already in use in confined, specialized areas such as factories and farms, and are being developed by a number of major manufacturers, including Volvo, Tesla, and Nissan. The sensors and computer programs involved have to process data in real-time to reliably navigate to your destination and control movement of the vehicle in relation to other road users. This involves prior creation of 3D maps of the routes to be used since the sensors cannot cope with non-mapped routes. Radar sensors are used to monitor other traffic, sending back data to an external central executive computer which controls the car. Sensors have to be programmed to detect shapes and distinguish between, for example, a child running into the road and a newspaper blowing across it; or to detect, say, an emergency traffic layout following an accident. However, these cars do not yet have the ability to react appropriately to all the problems posed by an ever-changing environment.

The first fatal crash involving an autonomous vehicle occurred in 2016, when neither the driver nor the autopilot reacted to a vehicle cutting across the car's path, meaning that the brakes were not applied. Tesla, the makers of the autonomous vehicle, in a June 2016 press release referred to the 'extremely rare circumstances of the impact'. The autopilot system warns drivers to keep their hands on the wheel at all times and even checks that they are doing so. Tesla state that this is the first fatality linked to their autopilot in 130 million miles of driving, compared with one fatality per 94 million miles of regular, non-automated driving in the US.

It has been estimated that each autonomous car will generate on average 30 Tb of data daily, much of which will have to be processed almost instantly. A new area of research, called *streaming analytics*, which bypasses traditional statistical and data processing methods, hopes to provide the means for dealing with this particular big data problem.

Astronomical data

In April 2014 an International Data Corporation report estimated that, by 2020, the digital universe will be 44 trillion *gigabytes*

(Gb; or 1,000 *megabytes* (Mb)), which is about ten times its size in 2013. An increasing volume of data is being produced by telescopes. For example, the Very Large Telescope in Chile is an optical telescope, which actually consists of four telescopes, each producing huge amounts of data—15 Tb per night, every night in total. It will spearhead the Large Synoptic Survey, a ten-year project repeatedly producing maps of the night sky, creating an estimated grand total of 60 Pb (2^{50} bytes).

Even bigger in terms of data generation is the Square Kilometer Array Pathfinder (ASKAP) radio telescope being built in Australia and South Africa, which is projected to begin operation in 2018. It will produce 160 Tb of raw data per second initially, and ever more as further phases are completed. Not all this data will be stored but even so, supercomputers around the world will be needed to analyse the remaining data.

What use is all this data?

It is now almost impossible to take part in everyday activities and avoid having some personal data collected electronically. Supermarket check-outs collect data on what we buy; airlines collect information about our travel arrangements when we purchase a ticket; and banks collect our financial data.

Big data is used extensively in commerce and medicine and has applications in law, sociology, marketing, public health, and all areas of natural science. Data in all its forms has the potential to provide a wealth of useful information if we can develop ways to extract it. New techniques melding traditional statistics and computer science make it increasingly feasible to analyse large sets of data. These techniques and algorithms developed by statisticians and computer scientists search for patterns in data. Determining which patterns are important is key to the success of big data analytics. The changes brought about by the digital age have substantially changed the way data is collected, stored, and analysed. The big data revolution has given us smart cars and home-monitoring.

The ability to gather data electronically resulted in the emergence of the exciting field of data science, bringing together the disciplines of statistics and computer science in order to analyse these large quantities of data to discover new knowledge in interdisciplinary areas of application. The ultimate aim of working with big data is to extract useful information. Decision-making in business, for example, is increasingly based on the information gleaned from big data, and expectations are high. But there are significant problems, not least with the shortage of trained data scientists capable of effectively developing and managing the systems necessary to extract the desired information.

By using new methods derived from statistics, computer science, and artificial intelligence, algorithms are now being designed that result in new insights and advances in science. For example, although it is not possible to predict exactly when and where an earthquake will occur, an increasing number of organizations are using data collected by satellite and ground sensors to monitor seismic activity. The aim is to determine approximately where big earthquakes are *likely* to occur in the long-term. For example, the US Geological Survey (USGS), a major player in seismic research, estimated in 2016 that 'there is a 76% probability that a magnitude 7 earthquake will occur within the next 30 years in northern California'. Probabilities such as these help focus resources on measures such as ensuring that buildings are better able to withstand earthquakes and having disaster management programmes in place. Several companies in these and other areas are working with big data to provide improved forecasting methods, which were not available before the advent of big data. We need to take a look at what is special about big data.

Chapter 2
Why is big data special?

Big data didn't just happen—it was closely linked to the development of computer technology. The rapid rate of growth in computing power and storage led to progressively more data being collected, and, regardless of who first coined the term, 'big data' was initially all about size. Yet it is not possible to define big data exclusively in terms of how many Pb, or even Eb, are being generated and stored. However, a useful means for talking about the 'big data' resulting from the data explosion is provided by the term 'small data'—although it is not widely used by statisticians. Big datasets are certainly large and complex, but in order for us to reach a definition, we need first to understand 'small data' and its role in statistical analysis.

Big data versus small data

In 1919, Ronald Fisher, now widely recognized as the founder of modern statistics as an academically rigorous discipline, arrived at Rothamsted Agricultural Experimental Station in the UK to work on analysing crop data. Data has been collected from the Classical Field Experiments conducted at Rothamsted since the 1840s, including both their work on winter wheat and spring barley and meteorological data from the field station. Fisher started the Broadbalk project which examined the effects of different fertilizers on wheat, a project still running today.

Recognizing the mess the data was in, Fisher famously referred to his initial work there as 'raking over the muck heap'. However, by meticulously studying the experimental results that had been carefully recorded in leather-bound note books he was able to make sense of the data. Working under the constraints of his time, before today's computing technology, Fisher was assisted only by a mechanical calculator as he, nonetheless successfully, performed calculations on seventy years of accumulated data. This calculator, known as the Millionaire, which relied for power on a tedious hand-cranking procedure, was innovative in its day, since it was the first commercially available calculator that could be used to perform multiplication. Fisher's work was computationally intensive and the Millionaire played a crucial role in enabling him to perform the many required calculations that any modern computer would complete within seconds.

Although Fisher collated and analysed a lot of data it would not be considered a large amount today, and it would certainly not be considered 'big data'. The crux of Fisher's work was the use of precisely defined and carefully controlled experiments, designed to produce highly structured, unbiased sample data. This was essential since the statistical methods then available could only be applied to structured data. Indeed, these invaluable techniques still provide the cornerstone for the analysis of small, structured sets of data. However, those techniques are not applicable to the very large amounts of data we can now access with so many different digital sources available to us.

Big data defined

In the digital age we are no longer entirely dependent on samples, since we can often collect all the data we need on entire populations. But the size of these increasingly large sets of data cannot alone provide a definition for the term 'big data'—we must include *complexity* in any definition. Instead of carefully constructed samples of 'small data' we are now dealing with huge amounts of data that has not been collected with any specific questions in mind and is often unstructured. In order to characterize the key features that make data big and move towards a definition of the term, Doug Laney, writing in 2001, proposed using the three 'v's: volume, variety, and velocity. By looking at each of these in turn we can get a better idea of what the term 'big data' means.

Volume

'Volume' refers to the amount of electronic data that is now collected and stored, which is growing at an ever-increasing rate. Big data is big, but how big? It would be easy just to set a specific size as denoting 'big' in this context, but what was considered 'big' ten years ago is no longer big by today's standards. Data acquisition is growing at such a rate that any chosen limit would inevitably soon become outdated. In 2012, IBM and the University of Oxford reported the findings of their Big Data Work Survey. In this international survey of 1,144 professionals working in ninety-five different countries, over half judged datasets of between 1 Tb and 1 Pb to be big, while about a third of respondents fell in the 'don't know' category. The survey asked respondents to choose either one or two defining characteristics of big data from a choice of eight; only 10 per cent voted for 'large volumes of data' with the top choice being 'a greater scope of information', which attracted 18 per cent. Another reason why there can be no definitive limit based solely on size is because other factors, like storage and the type of data being collected, change over time and affect our perception of volume. Of course, some datasets are very big indeed, including, for example, those obtained by the Large Hadron Collider at CERN, the world's premier particle accelerator, which has been operating since 2008. Even after extracting only 1 per cent of the total data generated, scientists still have 25 Pb to process annually. Generally, we can say the volume criterion is met if the dataset is such that we cannot collect, store, and analyse it using traditional computing and statistical methods. Sensor data, such as that generated by the Large Hadron Collider, is just one variety of big data, so let's consider some of the others.

Variety

Though you may often see the terms 'Internet' and 'World Wide Web' used interchangeably, they are actually very different. The Internet is a network of networks, consisting of computers, computer networks, local area networks (LANs), satellites, and cellphones and other electronic devices, all linked together and able to send bundles of data to one another, which they do using an IP (Internet protocol) address. The World Wide Web (www, or Web), described by its inventor, T. J. Berners-Lee, as 'a global information system', exploited Internet access so that all those with a computer and a connection could communicate with other users through such media as email, instant messaging, social networking, and texting. Subscribers to an ISP (Internet services provider) can connect to the Internet and so access the Web and many other services.

Once we are connected to the Web, we have access to a chaotic collection of data, from sources both reliable and suspect, prone to repetition and error. This is a long way from the clean and precise data demanded by traditional statistics. Although the data collected from the Web can be structured, unstructured, or semi-structured resulting in significant variety (e.g. unstructured word-processed documents or posts found on social networking sites; and semi-structured spreadsheets), most of the big data derived from the Web is unstructured. Twitter users, for example, publish approximately 500 million 140-character messages, or *tweets*, per day worldwide. These short messages are valuable commercially and are often analysed according to whether the sentiment expressed is positive, negative, or neutral. This new area of sentiment analysis requires specially developed techniques and is something we can do effectively only by using big data analytics. Although a great variety of data is collected by hospitals, the military, and many commercial enterprises for a number of purposes, ultimately it can all be classified as structured, unstructured, or semi-structured.

Velocity

Data is now streaming continuously from sources such as the Web, smartphones, and sensors. Velocity is necessarily connected with volume: the faster data is generated, the more there is. For example, the messages on social media that now 'go viral' are transmitted in such a way as to have a snowball effect: I post something on social media, my friends look at it, and each shares it with their friends, and so on. Very quickly these messages make their way around the world.

Velocity also refers to the speed at which data is electronically processed. For example, sensor data, such as that being generated by an autonomous car, is necessarily generated in real-time. If the car is to work reliably, the data, sent wirelessly to a central location, must be analysed very quickly so that the necessary instructions can be sent back to the car in a timely fashion.

Variability may be considered as an additional dimension of the velocity concept, referring to the changing rates in flow of data, such as the considerable increase in data flow during peak times. This is significant because computer systems are more prone to failure at these times.

Veracity

As well as the original three 'v's suggested by Laney, we may add 'veracity' as a fourth. Veracity refers to the quality of the data being collected. Data that is accurate and reliable has been the hallmark of statistical analysis in the past century. Fisher, and others, strived to devise methods encapsulating these two concepts, but the data generated in the digital age is often unstructured, and often collected without experimental design or, indeed, any concept of what questions might be of interest. And yet we seek to gain information from this mish-mash. Take, for example, the data generated by social networks. This data is by its very nature imprecise, uncertain, and often the information posted is simply not true. So how can we trust the data to yield meaningful results? Volume can help in overcoming these problems—as we saw in Chapter 1, when Thucydides described the Plataean forces engaging the greatest possible number of soldiers counting bricks in order to be more likely to get (close to) the correct height of the wall they wished to scale. However, we need to be more cautious, as we know from statistical theory, greater volume can lead to the opposite result, in that, given sufficient data, we can find any number of spurious correlations.

Visualization and other 'v's

'V' has become the letter of choice, with competing definitions adding or substituting such terms as 'vulnerability' and 'viability' to Laney's original three—the most important perhaps of these additions being 'value' and 'visualization'. Value generally refers to the quality of the results derived from big data analysis. It has also been used to describe the selling by commercial enterprises of data to firms who then process it using their own analytics, and so it is a term often referred to in the data business world.

Visualization is not a characterizing feature of big data, but it is important in the presentation and communication of analytic results. The familiar static pie charts and bar graphs that help us to understand small datasets have been further developed to aid in the visual interpretation of big data, but these are limited in their applicability. Infographics, for example, provide a more complex presentation but are static. Since big data is constantly being added to, the best visualizations are interactive for the user and updated regularly by the originator. For example, when we use GPS for planning a car journey, we are accessing a highly interactive graphic, based on satellite data, to track our position.

Taken together, the four main characteristics of big data—volume, variety, velocity, and veracity—present a considerable challenge in data management. The advantages we expect to gain from meeting this challenge and the questions we hope to answer with big data can be understood through data mining.

Big data mining

'Data is the new oil', a phrase that is common currency among leaders in industry, commerce, and politics, is usually attributed to Clive Humby in 2006, the originator of Tesco's customer loyalty card. It's a catchy phrase and suggests that data, like oil, is extremely valuable but must first be processed before that value can be realized. The phrase is primarily used as a marketing ploy by data analytics providers hoping to sell their products by convincing companies that big data is the future. It may well be, but the metaphor only holds so far. Once you strike oil you have a marketable commodity. Not so with big data; unless you have the right data you can produce nothing of value. Ownership is an issue; privacy is an issue; and, unlike oil, data appears not to be a finite resource. However, continuing loosely with the industrial metaphor, mining big data is the task of extracting useful and valuable information from massive datasets.

Using data mining and machine learning methods and algorithms, it is possible not only to detect unusual patterns or anomalies in data, but also to predict them. In order to acquire this kind of knowledge from big datasets, either supervised or unsupervised machine learning techniques may be used. Supervised machine learning can be thought of as roughly comparable to learning from example in humans. Using training data, where correct examples are labelled, a computer program develops a rule or algorithm for classifying new examples. This algorithm is checked using the test data. In contrast, unsupervised learning algorithms use unlabelled input data and no target is given; they are designed to explore data and discover hidden patterns.

As an example let's look at credit card fraud detection, and see how each method is used.

Credit card fraud detection

A lot of effort goes into detecting and preventing credit card fraud. If you have been unfortunate enough to receive a phone call from your credit card fraud detection office, you may be wondering how the decision was reached that the recently made purchase on your card had a good chance of being fraudulent. Given the huge number of credit card transactions it is no longer feasible to have humans checking transactions using traditional data analysis techniques, and so big data analytics are increasingly becoming necessary. Understandably, financial institutions are unwilling to share details of their fraud detection methods since doing so would give cyber criminals the information they need to develop ways round it. However, the broad brush strokes present an interesting picture.

There are several possible scenarios but we can look at personal banking and consider the case in which a credit card has been stolen and used in conjunction with other stolen information, such as the card PIN (personal identification number). In this case, the card might show a sudden increase in expenditure—a fraud that is easily detected by the card issuing agency. More often, a fraudster will first use a stolen card for a 'test transaction' in which something inexpensive is purchased. If this does not raise any alarms, then a bigger amount is taken. Such transactions may or may not be fraudulent—maybe a cardholder bought something outside of their usual purchasing pattern, or maybe they actually just spent a lot that month. So how do we detect which transactions are fraudulent? Let's look first at an unsupervised technique, called *clustering*, and how it might be used in this situation.

Clustering

Based on artificial intelligence algorithms, clustering methods can be used to detect anomalies in customer purchasing behaviour. We are looking for patterns in transaction data and want to detect anything unusual or suspicious which may or may not be fraudulent.

A credit card company gathers lots of data and uses it to form profiles showing the purchasing behaviour of their customers. Clusters of profiles with similar properties are then identified electronically using an *iterative* (i.e. repeating a process to generate a result) computer program. For example, a cluster may be defined on accounts with a typical spending range or location, a customer's upper spending limit, or on the kind of items purchased, each resulting in a separate cluster.

When data is collected by a credit card provider it does not carry any label indicating whether the transactions are genuine or fraudulent. Our task is to use this data as input and, using a suitable algorithm, accurately categorize transactions. To do this, we will need to find similar groups, or clusters, within the input data. So, for example, we might group data according to the amount spent, the location where the transaction took place, the kind of purchase made, or the age of the card holder. When a new transaction is made, the cluster identification is computed for that transaction and if it is different from the existing cluster identification for that customer, it is treated as suspicious. Even if it falls within the usual cluster, if it is sufficiently far from the centre of the cluster it may still arouse suspicion.

For example, say an 83-year-old grandmother living in Pasadena purchases a flashy sports car; if this does not cluster with her

Cluster A

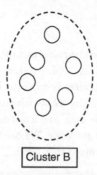

Cluster B

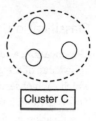

Cluster C

1. A cluster diagram.

usual purchasing behaviour of, say, groceries and visits to the
hairdresser, it would be considered anomalous. Anything out of
the ordinary, like this purchase, is considered worthy of further
investigation, usually starting by contacting the card owner. In
Figure 1 we see a very simple example of a cluster diagram
representing this situation.

Cluster B shows the grandmother's usual monthly expenditure
clustered with other people who have a similar monthly
expenditure. Now, in some circumstances, for example when
taking her annual vacation, the grandmother's expenditure for the
month increases, perhaps grouping her with those in Cluster C,
which is not too far distant from Cluster B and so not drastically
dissimilar. Even so, since it is in a different cluster, it would be
checked as suspicious account activity, but the purchase of the
flashy sports car on her account puts her expenditure into Cluster
A, which is very distant from her usual cluster and so is highly
unlikely to reflect a legitimate purchase.

In contrast to this situation, if we already have a set of examples
where we know fraud has occurred, instead of clustering
algorithms we can use classification methods, which provide
another data mining technique used for fraud detection.

Classification

Classification, a supervised learning technique, requires prior knowledge of the groups involved. We start with a dataset in which each observation is already correctly labelled or classified. This is divided into a *training set*, which enables us to build a classification model of the data, and a *test set*, which is used to check that the model is a good one. We can then use this model to classify new observations as they arise.

To illustrate classification, we will build a small decision tree for detecting credit card fraud.

To build our decision tree, let us suppose that credit card transaction data has been collected and transactions classified as genuine or fraudulent based on our historical knowledge are provided, as shown in Figure 2.

Using this data, we can build the decision tree shown in Figure 3, which will allow the computer to classify new transactions entering the system. We wish to arrive at one of the two possible transaction classifications, genuine or fraudulent, by asking a series of questions.

Was the card reported stolen or lost?	Was the item purchased unusual?	Was the customer phoned and asked if they made the purchase?	Classification
No	No		Genuine transaction
No	Yes	Yes	Genuine transaction
No	Yes	No	Fraudulent transaction
Yes			Fraudulent transaction

2. **Fraud dataset with known classifications.**

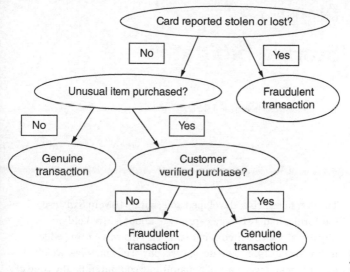

3. Decision tree for transactions.

By starting at the top of the tree in Figure 3, we have a series of test questions which will enable us to classify a new transaction

For example, if Mr Smith's account shows that he has reported his credit card as lost or stolen, then any attempt to use it is deemed fraudulent. If the card has not been reported lost or stolen, then the system will check to see if an unusual item or an item costing an unusual amount for this customer has been purchased. If not, then the transaction is seen as nothing out of the ordinary and labelled as genuine. On the other hand, if the item is unusual then a phone call to Mr Smith will be triggered. If he confirms that he did make the purchase, then it is deemed genuine; if not, fraudulent.

Having arrived at an informal definition of big data, and considered the kinds of questions that can be answered by mining big data, let us now turn to the problems of data storage.

Chapter 3
Storing big data

The first hard drive, developed and sold by IBM in San Jose, California, had a storage capacity of about 5 Mb, held on fifty disks, each 24 inches in diameter. This was cutting edge technology in 1956. The device was physically massive, weighed over 1 ton, and was part of a mainframe computer. By the time of the Apollo 11 moon landing in 1969, NASA's Manned Spacecraft Center in Houston was using mainframe computers that each had up to 8 Mb of memory. Amazingly, the onboard computer for the Apollo 11 moon landing craft, piloted by Neil Armstrong, had a mere 64 *kilobytes* (Kb) of memory.

Computer technology progressed rapidly and by the start of the personal computer boom in the 1980s, the average hard drive on a PC was 5 Mb when one was included, which was not always the case. This would hold one or two photos or images today. Computer storage capacity increased very quickly and although personal computer storage has not kept up with big data storage, it has increased dramatically in recent years. Now, you can buy a PC with an 8 Tb hard drive or even bigger. Flash drives are now available with 1 Tb of storage, which is sufficient to store approximately 500 hours of movies or over 300,000 photos. This seems a lot until we contrast it with the estimated 2.5 Eb of new data being generated every day.

Once the change from valves to transistors took place in the 1960s the number of transistors that could be placed on a chip grew very rapidly, roughly in accordance with Moore's Law, which we discuss in the next section. And despite predictions that the limit of miniaturization was about to be reached it continues to be a reasonable and useful approximation. We can now cram billions of increasingly faster transistors onto a chip, which allows us to store ever greater quantities of data, while multi-core processors together with multi-threading software make it possible to process that data.

Moore's Law

In 1965, Gordon Moore, who became the co-founder of Intel, famously predicted that over the next ten years the number of transistors incorporated in a chip would approximately double every twenty-four months. In 1975, he changed his prediction and suggested the complexity would double every twelve months for five years and then fall back to doubling every twenty-four months. David House, a colleague at Intel, after taking into account the increasing speed of transistors, suggested that the *performance* of microchips would double every eighteen months, and it is currently the latter prediction that is most often used for Moore's Law. This prediction has proved remarkably accurate; computers have indeed become faster, cheaper, and more powerful since 1965, but Moore himself feels that this 'law' will soon cease to hold.

According to M. Mitchell Waldrop in an article published in the February 2016 edition of the scientific journal *Nature*, the end is indeed nigh for Moore's Law. A microprocessor is the integrated circuit responsible for performing the instructions provided by a computer program. This usually consists of billions of transistors, embedded in a tiny space on a silicon microchip. A gate in each transistor allows it to be either switched on or off and so it can be used to store 0 and 1. A very small input current flows through each transistor gate and produces an amplified output current when the gate is closed. Mitchell Waldrop was interested in the distance between gates, currently at 14-nanometer gaps in top microprocessors, and stated that the problems of heat generation caused by closer circuitry and how it is to be effectively dissipated were causing the exponential growth predicted by Moore's Law to falter, which drew our attention to the fundamental limits he saw rapidly approaching.

A nanometre is 10^{-9} metre, or one-millionth of a millimetre. To put this in context, a human hair is about 75,000 nanometres in diameter and the diameter of an atom is between 0.1 and 0.5 nanometres. Paolo Gargini, who works for Intel, claimed that the gap limit will be 2 or 3 nanometres and will be reached in the not too distant future—maybe as soon as the 2020s. Waldrop speculates that 'at that scale, electron behaviour will be governed by quantum uncertainties that will make transistors hopelessly unreliable'. As we will see in Chapter 7, it seems quite likely that quantum computers, a technology still in its infancy, will eventually provide the way forward.

Moore's Law is now also applicable to the rate of growth for data as the amount generated appears to approximately double every two years. Data increases as storage capacity increases and the capacity to process data increases. We are all beneficiaries: Netflix, smartphones, the Internet of Things (IoT; a convenient way of referring to the vast numbers of electronic sensors connected to the Internet), and the Cloud (a worldwide network of interconnected servers) computing, among others, have all become possible because of the exponential growth predicted by Moore's Law. All this generated data has to be stored, and we look at this next.

Storing structured data

Anyone who uses a personal computer, laptop, or smartphone accesses data stored in a database. Structured data, such as bank statements and electronic address books, are stored in a relational database. In order to manage all this structured data, a relational database management system (RDBMS) is used to create, maintain, access, and manipulate the data. The first step is to design the database schema (i.e. the structure of the database). In order to achieve this, we need to know the data fields and be able to arrange them in tables, and we then need to identify the relationships between the tables. Once this has been accomplished and the database constructed we can populate it with data and interrogate it using structured query language (SQL).

Clearly tables have to be designed carefully and it would require a lot of work to make significant changes. However, the relational model should not be underestimated. For many structured data applications, it is fast and reliable. An important aspect of relational database design involves a process called *normalization* which includes reducing data duplication to a minimum and hence reduces storage requirements. This allows speedier queries, but even so as the volume of data increases the performance of these traditional databases decreases.

The problem is one of scalability. Since relational databases are essentially designed to run on just one server, as more and more data is added they become slow and unreliable. The only way to achieve scalability is to add more computing power, which has its limits. This is known as *vertical scalability*. So although structured data is usually stored and managed in an RDBMS, when the data is big, say in terabytes or petabytes and beyond, the RDBMS no longer works efficiently, even for structured data.

An important feature of relational databases and a good reason for continuing to use them is that they conform to the following group of properties: atomicity, consistency, isolation, and durability, usually known as ACID. Atomicity ensures that incomplete transactions cannot update the database; consistency excludes invalid data; isolation ensures one transaction does not interfere with another transaction; and durability means that the database must update before the next transaction is carried out. All these are desirable properties but storing and accessing big data, which is mostly unstructured, requires a different approach.

Unstructured data storage

For unstructured data, the RDBMS is inappropriate for several reasons, not least that once the relational database schema has been constructed, it is difficult to change it. In addition, unstructured data cannot be organized conveniently into rows and columns. As we have seen, big data is often high-velocity and generated in real-time with real-time processing requirements, so although the RDBMS is excellent for many purposes and serves us well, given the current data explosion there has been intensive research into new storage and management techniques.

In order to store these massive datasets, data is distributed across servers. As the number of servers involved increases, the chance of failure at some point also increases, so it is important to have multiple, reliably identical copies of the same data, each stored on a different server. Indeed, with the massive amounts of data now being processed, systems failure is taken as inevitable and so ways of coping with this are built into the methods of storage. So how are the needs for speed and reliability to be met?

Hadoop Distributed File System

A distributed file system (DFS) provides effective and reliable storage for big data across many computers. Influenced by the ideas published in October 2003 by Google in a research paper launching the Google File System, Doug Cutting, who was then working at Yahoo, and his colleague Mike Cafarella, a graduate student at the University of Washington, went to work on developing the Hadoop DFS. Hadoop, one of the most popular

DFS, is part of a bigger, open-source software project called the Hadoop Ecosystem. Named after a yellow soft toy elephant owned by Cutting's son, Hadoop is written in the popular programming language, Java. If you use Facebook, Twitter, or eBay, for example, Hadoop will have been working in the background while you do so. It enables the storage of both semi-structured and unstructured data, and provides a platform for data analysis.

When we use Hadoop DFS, the data is distributed across many nodes, often tens of thousands of them, physically situated in data centres around the world. Figure 4 shows the basic structure of a single Hadoop DFS cluster, which consists of one master NameNode and many slave DataNodes.

The NameNode deals with all requests coming in from a client computer; it distributes storage space, and keeps track of storage availability and data location. It also manages all the basic file operations (e.g. opening and closing files) and controls data access by client computers. The DataNodes are responsible for actually storing the data and in order to do so, create, delete, and replicate blocks as necessary.

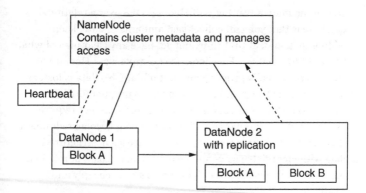

4. **Simplified view of part of a Hadoop DFS cluster.**

Data replication is an essential feature of the Hadoop DFS. For example, looking at Figure 4, we see that Block A is stored in both DataNode 1 and DataNode 2. It is important that several copies of each block are stored so that if a DataNode fails, other nodes are able to take over and continue with processing tasks without loss of data. In order to keep track of which DataNodes, if any, have failed, the NameNode receives a message from each, called a *Heartbeat*, every three seconds, and if no message is received it is assumed that the DataNode in question has ceased to function. So if DataNode 1 fails to send a Heartbeat, DataNode 2 will become the working node for Block A operations. The situation is different if the NameNode is lost, in which case the inbuilt backup system needs to be employed.

Data is written to a DataNode only once but will be read by an application many times. Each block is usually only 64 Mb, so there are a lot of them. One of the functions of the NameNode is to determine the best DataNode to use given the current usage, ensuring fast data access and processing. The client computer then accesses the data block from the chosen node. DataNodes are added as and when required by the increased storage requirements, a feature known as *horizontal scalability*.

One of the main advantages of Hadoop DFS over a relational database is that you can collect vast amounts of data, keep adding to it, and, at that time, not yet have any clear idea of what you want to use it for. Facebook, for example, uses Hadoop to store its continually growing amount of data. No data is lost, as it will store anything and everything in its original format. Adding DataNodes as required is cheap and does not require existing nodes to be changed. If previous nodes become redundant, it is easy to stop them working. As we have seen, structured data with identifiable rows and columns can be easily stored in a RDBMS while unstructured data can be stored cheaply and readily using a DFS.

NoSQL databases for big data

NoSQL is the generic name used to refer to non-relational databases and stands for *Not only SQL*. Why is there a need for a non-relational model that does not use SQL? The short answer is that the non-relational model allows us to continually add new data. The non-relational model has some features that are necessary in the management of big data, namely scalability, availability, and performance. With a relational database you cannot keep scaling vertically without loss of function, whereas with NoSQL you scale horizontally and this enables performance to be maintained. Before describing the NoSQL distributed database infrastructure and why it is suitable for big data, we need to consider the CAP Theorem.

CAP Theorem

In 2000, Eric Brewer, a professor of computer science at the University of California Berkeley, presented the CAP (consistency, availability, and partition tolerance) Theorem. Within the context of a distributed database system, consistency refers to the requirement that all copies of data should be the same across nodes. So in Figure 4, for example, Block A in DataNode 1 should be the same as Block A in DataNode 2. Availability requires that if a node fails, other nodes still function—if DataNode 1 fails, then DataNode 2 must still operate. Data, and hence DataNodes, are distributed across physically separate servers and communication between these machines will sometimes fail. When this occurs it is called a *network partition*. Partition tolerance requires that the system continues to operate even if this happens.

In essence, what the CAP Theorem states is that for any distributed computer system, where the data is shared, only two of these three criteria can be met. There are therefore three possibilities; the system must be: consistent and available, consistent and partition tolerant, or partition tolerant and available. Notice that since in a RDMS the network is not partitioned, only consistency and availability would be of concern and the RDMS model meets both of these criteria. In NoSQL, since we necessarily have partitioning, we have to choose between consistency and availability. By sacrificing availability, we are able to wait until consistency is achieved. If we choose instead to sacrifice consistency it follows that sometimes the data will differ from server to server.

The somewhat contrived acronym BASE (Basically Available, Soft, and Eventually consistent) is used as a convenient way of describing this situation. BASE appears to have been chosen in contrast to the ACID properties of relational databases. 'Soft' in this context refers to the flexibility in the consistency requirement. The aim is not to abandon any one of these criteria but to find a way of optimizing all three, essentially a compromise.

The architecture of NoSQL databases

The name NoSQL derives from the fact that SQL cannot be used to query these databases. So, for example, joins such as the one we saw in Figure 4 are not possible. There are four main types of non-relational or NoSQL database: key–value, column-based, document, and graph—all useful for storing large amounts of structured and semi-structured data. The simplest is the key–value database, which consists of an identifier (the *key*) and the data associated with that key (the *value*) as shown in Figure 5. Notice that 'value' can contain multiple items of data.

Of course, there would be many such key–value pairs and adding new ones or deleting old ones is simple enough, making the database highly scalable horizontally. The primary capability is that we can look up the value for a given key. For example, using the key 'Jane Smith' we are able to find her address. With huge amounts of data, this provides a fast, reliable, and readily scalable solution to storage

Key	Value
Jane Smith	Address: 33 Any Drive; Any City
Tom Brown	Gender: Male; Marital Status: Married; # of Children: 2; Favourite Movies: Cinderella; Dracula; Patton

5. Key–value database.

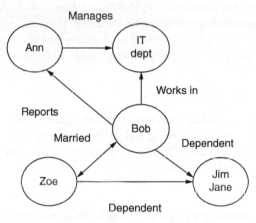

6. Graph database.

but it is limited by not having a query language. Column-based and document databases are extensions of the key–value model.

Graph databases follow a different model and are popular with social networking sites as well as being useful in business applications. These graphs are often very large, particularly when used by social networking sites. In this kind of database, the information is stored in nodes (i.e. vertices) and edges. For example, the graph in Figure 6 shows five nodes with the arrows between them representing relationships. Adding, updating, or deleting nodes changes the graph.

In this example, the nodes are names or departments, and the edges are the relationships between them. Data is retrieved from the graph by looking at the edges. So, for example, if I want to find 'names of employees in the IT department who have dependent children', I see that Bob fulfils both criteria. Notice that this is not a directed graph—we do not follow the arrows, we look for links.

Currently, an approach called NewSQL is finding a niche. By combining the performance of NoSQL databases and the ACID properties of the relational model, the aim of this latent technology is to solve the scalability problems associated with the relational model, making it more useable for big data.

Cloud storage

Like so many modern computing terms the Cloud sounds friendly, comforting, inviting, and familiar, but actually 'the Cloud' is, as mentioned earlier, just a way of referring to a network of interconnected servers housed in data centres across the world. These data centres provide a hub for storing big data.

Through the Internet we share the use of these remote servers, provided (on payment of a fee) by various companies, to store and manage our files, to run apps, and so on. As long as your computer or other device has the requisite software to access the Cloud, you can view your files from anywhere and give permission for others to do so. You can also use software that 'resides' in the Cloud rather than on your computer. So it's not just a matter of accessing the Internet but also of having the means to store and process information—hence the term 'Cloud computing'. Our individual Cloud storage needs are not that big, but scaled up the amount of information stored is massive.

Amazon is the biggest provider of Cloud services but the amount of data managed by them is a commercial secret. We can get some idea of their importance in Cloud computing by looking at an incident that occurred in February 2017 when Amazon Web Services' Cloud storage system, S3, suffered a major *outage* (i.e. service was lost). This lasted for approximately five hours and resulted in the loss of connection to many websites and services, including Netflix, Expedia, and the US Securities and Exchange Commission. Amazon later reported human error as the cause, stating that one of their employees had been responsible for inadvertently taking servers offline. Rebooting these large systems took longer than expected but was eventually completed successfully. Even so, the incident highlights the susceptibility of the Internet to failure, whether by a genuine mistake or by ill-intentioned hacking.

Lossless data compression

In 2017, the widely respected International Data Corporation (IDC) estimates that the digital universe totals a massive 16 *zettabytes* (Zb) which amounts to an unfathomable 16×10^{21} bytes. Ultimately, as the digital universe continues to grow, questions concerning what data we should actually save, how many copies should be kept, and for how long will have to be addressed. It rather challenges the *raison d'être* of big data to consider purging data stores on a regular basis or even archiving them, as this is in itself costly and potentially valuable data could be lost given that we do not necessarily know what data might be important to us in the future. However, with the huge amounts of data being stored, data compression has become necessary in order to maximize storage space.

There is considerable variability in the quality of the data collected electronically and so before it can be usefully analysed it must be pre-processed to check for and remedy problems with consistency, repetition, and reliability. Consistency is clearly important if we are to rely on the information extracted from the data. Removing unwanted repetitions is good housekeeping for any dataset, but with big datasets there is the additional concern that there may not be sufficient storage space available to keep all the data. Data is compressed to reduce redundancy in videos and images and so reduce storage requirements and, in the case of videos, to improve streaming rates.

There are two main types of compression—lossless and lossy. In *lossless compression* all the data is preserved and so this is particularly useful for text. For example, files with the extension '.ZIP', have been compressed without loss of information so that unzipping them returns us to the original file. If we compress the string of characters 'aaaaabbbbbbbbbb' as '5a10b' it is easy to see how to decompress and arrive at the original string. There are many algorithms for compression but it is useful first to consider how data is stored without compression.

ASCII (American Standard Code for Information Interchange) is the standard way of encoding data so that it can be stored in a computer. Each character is designated a decimal number, its ASCII code. As we have already seen, data is stored as a series of 0s and 1s. These binary digits are called *bits*. Standard ASCII uses 8 bits (also defined as 1 byte) to store each character. For example, in ASCII the letter 'a' is denoted by the decimal number 97 which converts to 01100001 in binary. These values are looked up in the standard ASCII table, a small part of which is given at the end of the book. Upper-case letters have different ASCII codes.

Consider the character string 'added' which is shown coded in Figure 7.

Character string	a	d	d	e	d
ASCII	97	100	100	101	100
Binary	01100001	01100100	01100100	01100101	01100100

7. **A coded character string.**

So 'added' takes 5 bytes or 5 * 8 = 40 bits of storage. Given Figure 7, decoding is accomplished using the ASCII code table. This is not an economical way of encoding and storing data; 8 bits per character seems excessive and no account is taken of the fact that in text documents some letters are used much more frequently than others. There are many lossless data compression models, such as the Huffman algorithm, which uses less storage space by variable length encoding, a technique based on how often a particular letter occurs. Those letters with the highest occurrence are given shorter codes.

Taking the string 'added' again we note that 'a' occurs once, 'e' occurs once, and 'd' occurs three times. Since 'd' occurs most frequently, it should be assigned the shortest code. To find the Huffman code for each letter we count the letters of 'added' as follows:

$$1a \to 1e \to 3d$$

Next, we find the two letters that occur least frequently, namely 'a' and 'e', and we form the structure in Figure 8, called a *binary tree*. The number 2 at the top of the tree is found by adding the number of occurrences of the two least frequent letters.

In Figure 9, we show the new node representing three occurrences of the letter 'd'.

Figure 9 shows the completed tree with total number of letter occurrences at the top. Each edge of the tree is coded as either

8. A binary tree.

9. The binary tree with a new node.

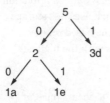

Letter	Code (bits)
a	00
e	10
d	1

10. Completed binary tree.

0 or 1, as shown in Figure 10, and the codes are found by following the paths up the tree.

So 'added' is coded as a = 00, d = 1, d = 1, e = 10, d = 1, which gives us 0011101. Using this method we see that 3 bits are used for storing the letter 'd', 2 bits for letter 'a', and 2 bits for letter 'e', giving a total of 7 bits. This is a big improvement on the original 40 bits.

A way of measuring the efficiency of compression is to use the data compression ratio, which is defined as the uncompressed size of a file divided by its compressed size. In this example, 45/7 is approximately equal to 6.43, a high compression rate, showing good storage savings. In practice these trees are very large and are optimized using sophisticated mathematical techniques. This example has shown how we can compress data without losing any of the information contained in the original file and it is therefore called lossless compression.

Lossy data compression

In comparison, sound and image files are usually much larger than text files and so another technique called *lossy compression* is used. This is because, when we are dealing with sound and images, lossless compression methods may simply not result in a sufficiently high compression ratio for data storage to be viable. Equally, some data loss is tolerable for sound and images. Lossy compression exploits this latter feature by permanently removing some data in the original file so reducing the amount of storage space needed. The basic idea is to remove some of the detail without overly affecting our perception of the image or sound.

For example, consider a black and white photograph, more correctly described as a *greyscale image*, of a child eating an ice-cream at the seaside. Lossy compression removes an equal amount of data from the image of the child and that of the sea. The percentage of data removed is calculated such that it will not have a significant impact on the viewer's perception of the resulting (compressed) image—too much compression will lead to a fuzzy photo. There's a trade-off between the level of compression and quality of picture.

If we want to compress a greyscale image, we first divide it into blocks of 8 pixels by 8 pixels. Since this is a very small area, all the pixels are generally similar in tone. This observation, together with knowledge about how we perceive images, is fundamental to lossy compression. Each pixel has a corresponding numeric value between 0 for pure black and 255 for pure white, with the numbers between representing shades of grey. After some further processing using a method called the Discrete Cosine Algorithm, an average intensity value for each block is found and the results compared with each of the actual values in a given block. Since we are comparing these actual values to the average most of them will be 0, or 0 when rounded. Our lossy algorithm collects all these 0s together, which represent the information from the pixels that is less important to the image. These values, corresponding to high frequencies in our image, are all grouped together and the redundant information is removed, using a technique called *quantization*, resulting in compression. For example if out of sixty-four values each requiring 1 byte of storage, we have twenty 0s, then after compression we need only 45 bytes of storage. This process is repeated for all the blocks that make up the image and so redundant information is removed throughout.

For colour images the JPEG (Joint Photographic Experts Group) algorithm, for example, recognizes red, blue, and green, and assigns each a different weight based on the known properties of human visual perception. Green is weighted greatest since the human eye is more perceptive to green than to red or blue. Each pixel in a colour image is assigned a red, blue, and green weighting, represented as a triple <R,G,B>. For technical reasons, <R,G,B> triples are usually converted into another triple, <YCbCr> where Y represents the intensity of the colour and both Cb and Cr are chrominance values, which describe the actual colour. Using a complex mathematical algorithm it is possible to reduce the values of each pixel and ultimately achieve lossy compression by reducing the number of pixels saved.

Multimedia files in general, because of their size, are compressed using lossy methods. The more compressed the file, the poorer the reproduction quality, but because some of the data is sacrificed, greater compression ratios are achievable, making the file smaller.

Following an international standard for image compression first produced in 1992 by the JPEG, the JPEG file format provides the most popular method for compressing both colour and greyscale photographs. This group is still very active and meets several times a year.

Consider again the example of a black and white photograph of a child eating an ice-cream at the seaside. Ideally, when we compress this image we want the part featuring the child to remain sharp, so in order to achieve this we would be willing to sacrifice some clarity in the background details. A new method, called *data warping compression*, developed by researchers at

Henry Samueli School of Engineering and Applied Science, UCLA, now makes this possible. Those readers interested in the details are referred to the Further reading section at the end of the book.

We have seen how a distributed data file system can be used to store big data. Problems with storage have been overcome to the extent that big data sources can now be used to answer questions that previously we could not answer. As we will see in Chapter 4, an algorithmic method called *MapReduce* is used for processing data stored in the Hadoop DFS.

Chapter 4
Big data analytics

Having discussed how big data is collected and stored, we can now look at some of the techniques used to discover useful information from that data such as customer preferences or how fast an epidemic is spreading. Big data analytics, the catch-all term for these techniques, is changing rapidly as the size of the datasets increases and classical statistics makes room for this new paradigm.

Hadoop, introduced in Chapter 3, provides a means for storing big data through its distributed file system. As an example of big data analytics we'll look at MapReduce, which is a distributed data processing system and forms part of the core functionality of the Hadoop Ecosystem. Amazon, Google, Facebook, and many other organizations use Hadoop to store and process their data.

MapReduce

A popular way of dealing with big data is to divide it up into small chunks and then process each of these individually, which is basically what MapReduce does by spreading the required calculations or queries over many, many computers. It's well worth working through a much simplified and reduced example of how MapReduce works—and as we are doing this by hand it really will need to be a considerably reduced example, but it will still demonstrate the process that would be used for big data. There would be typically many thousands of processors used to process a huge amount of data in parallel, but the process is scalable and it's actually a very ingenious idea and simple to follow.

There are several parts to this analytics model: the *map* component; the *shuffle* step; and the *reduce* component. The map component is written by the user and sorts the data we are interested in. The shuffle step, which is part of the main Hadoop MapReduce code, then groups the data by key, and finally we have the reduce component, which again is provided by the user, which aggregates these groups and produces the result. The result is then sent to HDFS for storage.

For example, suppose we have the following key–value files stored in the Hadoop distributed file system, with statistics on each of the following: measles, Zika virus, TB, and Ebola. The disease is the key and a value representing the number of cases for each disease is given. We are interested in the total number of cases of each disease.

File 1:
Measles,3
Zika,2 TB,1 Measles,1
Zika,3 Ebola,2

File 2:
Measles,4
Zika,2 TB,1

File 3:
Measles,3 Zika,2
Measles,4 Zika,1 Ebola,3

The mapper enables us to read each of these input files separately, line by line, as shown in Figure 11. The mapper then returns the key–value pairs for each of these distinct lines.

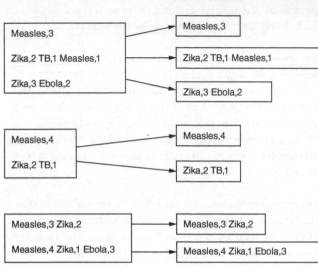

11. Map function.

Having split the files and found key–values for each split, the
next step in the algorithm is provided by the master program,
which sorts and shuffles the key–values. The diseases are sorted
alphabetically and the result is sent to an appropriate file ready
for the reducer, as shown in Figure 12.

Continuing to follow Figure 12, the reduce component combines
the results of the map and shuffle stages, and as a result sends
each disease to a separate file. The reduce step in the algorithm
then allows the individual totals to be calculated and these results
are sent to a final output file, as key–value pairs, which can be
saved in the DFS.

This is a very small example, but the MapReduce method enables
us to analyse very large amounts of data. For example, using the
data supplied by Common Crawl, a non-profit organization that

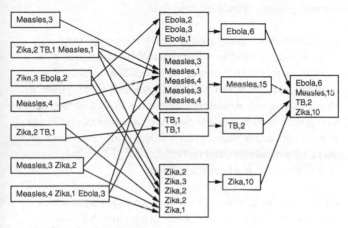

12. Shuffle and reduce functions.

provides a free copy of the Internet, we could count the number of times each word occurs on the Internet by writing a suitable computer program that uses MapReduce.

Bloom filters

A particularly useful method for mining big data is the Bloom filter, a technique based on probability theory which was developed in the 1970s. As we will see, Bloom filters are particularly suited to applications where storage is an issue and where the data can be thought of as a list.

The basic idea behind Bloom filters is that we want to build a system, based on a list of data elements, to answer the question 'Is X in the list?' With big datasets, searching through the entire set may be too slow to be useful, so we use a Bloom filter which, being a probabilistic method, is not 100 per cent accurate—the algorithm may decide that an element belongs to the list when actually it does not; but it is a fast, reliable, and storage efficient method of extracting useful knowledge from data.

Bloom filters have many applications. For example, they can be used to check whether a particular Web address leads to a malicious website. In this case, the Bloom filter would act as a blacklist of known malicious URLs against which it is possible to check, quickly and accurately, whether it is likely that the one you have just clicked on is safe or not. Web addresses newly found to be malicious can be added to the blacklist. Since there are now over a billion websites, and more being added daily, keeping track of malicious sites is a big data problem.

A related example is that of malicious email messages, which may be spam or may contain phishing attempts. A Bloom filter provides us with a quick way of checking each email address and hence we would be able to issue a timely warning if appropriate. Each address occupies approximately 20 bytes, so storing and checking each of them becomes prohibitively time-consuming since we need to do this very quickly—by using a Bloom filter we are able to reduce the amount of stored data dramatically. We can see how this works by following the process of building a small Bloom filter and showing how it would function.

Suppose we have the following list of email addresses that we want to flag as malicious: <aaa@aaaa.com>; <bbb@nnnn.com>; <ccc@ff.com>; <dd@ggg.com>. To build our Bloom filter first assume we have 10 bits of memory available on a computer. This is called a *bit array* and initially it is empty. A bit has just two states, usually denoted by 0 and 1, so we will start by setting all values in the bit array to 0, meaning empty. As we will see shortly, a bit with a value of 1 will mean the associated index has been assigned at least once.

The size of our bit array is fixed and will remain the same regardless of how many cases we add. We index each bit in the array as shown in Figure 13.

Index	0	1	2	3	4	5	6	7	8	9
Bit value	0	0	0	0	0	0	0	0	0	0

13. 10-bit array.

We now need to introduce *hash functions*, which are algorithms designed to map each element in a given list to one of the positions in the array. By doing this, we now store only the mapped position in the array, rather than the email address itself, so that the amount of storage space required is reduced.

For our demonstration, we show the result of using two hash functions, but typically seventeen or eighteen functions would be used together with a much bigger array. Since these functions are designed to map more or less uniformly, each index has an equal chance of being the result each time the hash algorithm is applied to a different address.

So, first we let the hash algorithms assign each email address to one of the indices of the array.

To add 'aaa@aaaa.com' to the array, it is first passed through hash function 1, which returns an array index or position value. For example, let's say hash function 1 returned index 3. Hash function 2, again applied to 'aaa@aaaa.com', returned index 4. These two positions will each have their stored bit value set to 1. If the position was already set to 1 then it would be left alone. Similarly, adding 'bbb@nnnn.com' may result in positions 2 and 7 being occupied or set to 1 or 'ccc@ff.com' may return positions 4 and 7. Finally, assume the hash functions applied to 'dd@ggg.com' return the positions 2 and 6. These results are summarized in Figure 14.

The actual Bloom filter array is shown in Figure 15 with occupied positions having a value set to 1.

DATA	HASH 1	HASH 2
aaa@aaaa.com	3	4
bbb@nnnn.com	2	7
ccc@ff.com	4	7
dd@ggg.com	2	6

14. Summary of hash function results.

Index	0	1	2	3	4	5	6	7	8	9
Bit value	0	0	1	1	1	0	1	1	0	0

15. Bloom filter for malicious email addresses.

So, how do we use this array as a Bloom filter? Suppose, now, that we receive an email and we wish to check whether the address appears on the malicious email address list. Suppose it maps to positions 2 and 7, both of which have value 1. Because all values returned are equal to 1 it *probably* belongs to the list and so is *probably* malicious. We cannot say for certain that it belongs to the list because positions 2 and 7 have been the result of mapping other addresses and indexes may be used more than once. So the result of testing an element for list membership also includes the probability of returning a false positive. However, if an array index with value 0 is returned by any hash function (and, remember, there would generally be seventeen or eighteen functions) we would then definitely know that the address was not on the list.

The mathematics involved is complex but we can see that the bigger the array the more unoccupied spaces there will be and the less chance of a false positive result or incorrect matching. Obviously the size of the array will be determined by the number of keys and hash functions used, but it must be big enough to allow a sufficient number of unoccupied spaces for the filter to function effectively and minimize the number of false positives.

Bloom filters are fast and they can provide a very useful way of detecting fraudulent credit card transactions. The filter checks to see whether or not a particular item belongs to a given list or set, so an unusual transaction would be flagged as not belonging to the list of your usual transactions. For example if you have never purchased mountaineering equipment on your credit card, a Bloom filter will flag the purchase of a climbing rope as suspicious. On the other hand, if you do buy mountaineering equipment, the Bloom filter will identify this purchase as probably acceptable but there will be a probability that the result is actually false.

Bloom filters can also be used for filtering email for spam. Spam filters provide a good example since we do not know exactly what we are looking for—often we are looking for patterns, so if we want email messages containing the word 'mouse' to be treated as spam we also want variations like 'mOuse' and 'mou$e' to be treated as spam. In fact, we want all possible, identifiable variations of the word to be identified as spam. It is much easier to filter everything that does not match with a given word, so we would only allow 'mouse' to pass through the filter.

Bloom filters are also used to speed up the algorithms used for Web query rankings, a topic of considerable interest to those who have websites to promote.

PageRank

When we search on Google, the websites returned are ranked according to their relevance to the search terms. Google achieves this ordering primarily by applying an algorithm called PageRank. The name PageRank is popularly believed to have been chosen after Larry Page, one of the founders of Google, who, working with co-founder Sergey Brin, published articles on this new algorithm. Until the summer of 2016, PageRank results were publicly available by downloading the Toolbar PageRank. The public PageRank tool was based on a range from 1 and 10. Before it was withdrawn, I saved a few results. If I typed 'Big Data' into Google using my laptop, I got a message informing me there were 'About 370,000,000 results (0.44 seconds)' with a PageRank of 9. Top of this list were some paid advertisements, followed by Wikipedia. Searching on 'data' returned about 5,530,000,000 results in 0.43 seconds with a PageRank of 9. Other examples, all with a PageRank of 10, included the USA government website, Facebook, Twitter, and the European University Association.

This method of calculating a PageRank is based on the number of links pointing to a webpage—the more links, the higher the score, and the higher the page appears as a search result. It does not reflect the number of times a page is visited. If you are a website designer, you want to optimize your website so that it appears very near the top of the list given certain search terms, since most people do not look further than the first three or four results. This requires a huge number of links and as a result, almost inevitably, a trade in links became established. Google tried to address this 'artificial' ranking by assigning a new ranking of 0 to implicated companies or even by removing them completely from Google, but this did not solve the problem; the trade was merely forced underground, and links continued to be sold.

PageRank itself has not been abandoned and forms part of a large suite of ranking programs which are not available for public viewing. Google re-calculates rankings regularly in order to reflect added links as well as new websites. Since PageRank is commercially sensitive, full details are not publicly available but we can get the general idea by looking at an example. The algorithm provides a complex way of analysing the links between webpages based on probability theory, where probability 1 indicates certainty and probability 0 indicates impossibility, with everything else having a probability value somewhere in-between.

To understand how the ranking works, we first need to know what a probability distribution looks like. If we think of the result of rolling a fair six-sided die, each of the outcomes 1 through 6 is equally likely to occur and so each has a probability of 1/6. The list of all the possible outcomes, together with the probability associated with each, describes a probability distribution.

Going back to our problem of ranking webpages according to importance, we cannot say that each is equally important, but if we had a way of assigning probabilities to each webpage, this would give us a reasonable indication of importance. So what algorithms such as PageRank do is construct a probability distribution for the entire Web. To explain this, let's consider a random surfer of the Web, who starts at any webpage and then moves to another page using the links available.

We will consider a simplified example where we have a web consisting of only three webpages; BigData1, BigData2, and BigData3. Suppose the only links are from BigData2 to BigData3, BigData2 to BigData1, and BigData1 to BigData3. Then our web can be represented as shown in Figure 16, where the nodes are webpages and the arrows (edges) are links.

Each page has a PageRank indicating its importance or popularity. BigData3 will be the most highly ranked because it has the most links going to it, making it the most popular. Suppose now that

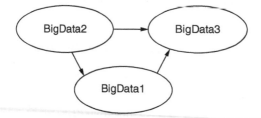

16. **Directed graph representing a small part of the Web.**

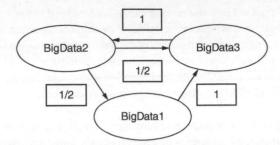

17. Directed graph representing a small part of the Web with added link.

a random surfer visits a webpage, he or she has one proportional vote to cast, which is divided equally between the next choices of webpage. For example, if our random surfer is currently visiting BigData1, the only choice is to then visit BigData3. So we can say that a vote of 1 is cast for BigData3 by BigData1.

In the real Web new links are made all the time, so suppose we now find that BigData3 links to BigData2, as shown in Figure 17, then the PageRank for BigData2 will have changed because the random surfer now has a choice of where to go after BigData3.

If our random surfer starts off at BigData1, then the only choice is to visit BigData3 next and so the total vote of 1 goes to BigData3, and BigData2 gets a vote of 0. If he or she starts at BigData2 the vote is split equally between BigData3 and BigData1. Finally, if the random surfer starts at BigData3 his or her entire vote is cast for BigData2. These proportional 'votes' are summarized in the Figure 18.

Using Figure 18, we now see the total votes cast for each webpage as follows:

Total votes for BD1 are 1/2 (coming from BD2)
Total votes for BD2 are 1 (coming from BD3)
Total votes for BD3 are 1½ (coming from BD 1 and BD2)

	Proportion of vote cast by BD1	Proportion of vote cast by BD2	Proportion of vote cast by BD3
For BD1	0	1/2	0
For BD2	0	0	1
For BD3	1	1/2	0

18. Votes cast for each webpage.

Since the choice of starting page for the surfer is random, each one is equally likely and so is assigned an initial PageRank of 1/3. To form the desired PageRanks for our example, we need to update the initial PageRanks according to the proportion of votes cast for each page.

For example, BD1 has just 1/2 vote, cast by BD2, so the PageRank of BD1 is $1/3 * 1/2 = 1/6$. Similarly, PageRank BD2 is given by $1/3 * 1 = 2/6$ and PageRank BD3 is $1/3 * 3/2 = 3/6$. Since all the Page Rankings now add up to one, we have a probability distribution which shows the importance, or rank, of each page.

But there is a complication here. We said that the probability that a random surfer was on any page initially was 1/3. After one step, we have calculated the probability that a random surfer is on BD1 is 1/6. What about after two steps? Well, again we use the current PageRanks as votes to calculate the new PageRanks. The calculations are slightly different for this round because the current PageRanks are not equal but the method is the same, giving new PageRanks as follows: PageRank BD1 is 2/12, PageRank BD2 is 6/12, and PageRank BD3 is 4/12. These steps, or iterations, are repeated until the algorithm converges, meaning that the process continues like this until no more changes can be made by any further multiplication. Having achieved a final ranking, PageRank can select the page with the highest ranking for a given search.

Page and Brin, in their original research papers, presented an equation for calculating the PageRank which included a Damping Factor d, defined as the probability that a random Web surfer will click on one of the links on the current page. The probability that a random Web surfer will *not* click on one of the links on the current page is therefore $(1 - d)$, meaning that the random surfer has finished surfing. It was this Damping Factor that ensured the PageRank averaged over the entire Web settles down to 1, after a sufficient number of iterative calculations. Page and Brin reported that a web consisting of 322 million links settled down after fifty-two iterations.

Public datasets

There are many freely available big datasets that interested groups or individuals can use for their own projects. Common Crawl, mentioned earlier in this chapter, is one example. Hosted by the Amazon Public Datasets Program, in October 2016 the Common Crawl monthly archive contained more than 3.25 billion webpages. Public datasets are in a broad range of specialties, including genome data, satellite imagery, and worldwide news data. For those not likely to write their own code, Google's Ngram Viewer provides an interesting way of exploring some big datasets interactively (see Further reading for details).

Big data paradigm

We have seen some of the ways in which big data can be useful and in Chapter 2 we talked about small data. For small data analysis, the scientific method is well-established and necessarily involves human interaction: someone comes up with an idea, formulates a hypothesis or model, and devises ways to test its predictions. Eminent statistician George Box wrote in 1978, 'all models are wrong, but some are useful'. The point he makes is that statistical and scientific models in general do not provide exact representations of the world about us, but a good model can provide a useful picture on which to base predictions and draw conclusions confidently. However, as we have shown, when working with big data we do not follow this method. Instead we find that the machine, not the scientist, is predominant.

Writing in 1962, Thomas Kuhn described the concept of scientific revolutions, which follow long periods of normal science when an existing paradigm is developed and investigated to the full. If sufficiently intractable anomalies occur to undermine the existing theory, resulting in loss of confidence by researchers, then this is termed a 'crisis', and it is ultimately resolved by a new theory or paradigm. For a new paradigm to be accepted, it must answer some of the questions found to be problematic in the old paradigm. However, in general, a new paradigm does not completely overwhelm the previous one. For example, the shift from Newtonian mechanics to Einstein's relativity theory changed the way science viewed the world, without making Newton's laws obsolete: Newtonian mechanics now form a special case of the wider ranging relativity theory. Shifting from classical statistics to big data analytics also represents a significant change, and has many of the hallmarks of a paradigm shift. So techniques will inevitably need to be developed to deal with this new situation.

Consider the technique of finding correlations in data, which provides a means of prediction based on the strength of the relationships between variables. It is acknowledged in classical statistics that correlation does not imply causation. For example, a teacher may document both the number of student absences from lectures and student grades; and then, on finding an apparent correlation, he or she may use absences to predict grades. However, it would be incorrect to conclude that absences cause poor grades. We cannot know why the two variables are correlated just by looking at the blind calculations: maybe the less able students tend to miss class; maybe students who are absent due to sickness cannot later catch up. Human interaction and interpretation is needed in order to decide which correlations are useful.

With big data, using correlation creates additional problems. If we consider a massive dataset, algorithms can be written that, when applied, return a large number of spurious correlations that are totally independent of the views, opinions, or hypotheses of any human being. Problems arise with false correlations—for example, divorce rate and margarine consumption, which is just one of many spurious correlations reported in the media. We can see the absurdity of this correlation by applying scientific method. However, when the number of variables becomes large, the number of spurious correlations also increases. This is one of the main problems associated with trying to extract useful information from big data, because in doing so, as with mining big data, we are usually looking for patterns and correlations. As we will see in Chapter 5, one of the reasons Google Flu Trends failed in its predictions was because of these problems.

Chapter 5
Big data and medicine

Big data analysis is significantly changing the world of healthcare. Its potential has yet to be fully realized but includes medical diagnosis, epidemic prediction, gauging the public response to government health warnings, and the reduction in costs associated with healthcare systems. Let's start by looking at what is now termed *healthcare informatics*.

Healthcare informatics

Medical big data is collected, stored, and analysed using the general techniques described in previous chapters. Broadly speaking, healthcare informatics and its many sub-disciplines, such as clinical informatics and bio-informatics, use big data to provide improved patient care and reduce costs. Consider the definition criteria for big data (discussed in Chapter 2)—volume, variety, velocity, and veracity—and how they apply to medical data. Volume and velocity are satisfied, for example, when public-health-related data is collected through social networking sites for epidemic tracking; variety is satisfied since patient records are stored in text format, both structured and unstructured, and sensor data such as that provide by MRIs is also collected; veracity is fundamental to medical applications and considerable care is taken to eliminate inaccurate data.

Social media is a potentially valuable source of medically related information through data collection from sites such as Facebook, Twitter, various blogs, message boards, and Internet searches. Message boards focused on specific healthcare issues are abundant, providing a wealth of unstructured data. Posts on both Facebook and Twitter have been mined, using classification techniques similar to those described in Chapter 4, to monitor experience of unpleasant reactions to medications and supply healthcare professionals with worthwhile information regarding drug interactions and drug abuse. Mining social media data for public-health-related research is now a recognized practice within the academic community.

Designated social networking sites for medical professionals, such as Sermo Intelligence, a worldwide medical network and self-proclaimed 'largest global healthcare data collection company', provide healthcare personnel with instant crowdsourcing benefits from interaction with their peers. Online medical advice sites are becoming increasingly popular and generate yet more information. But, although not publicly accessible, perhaps the most important source is the vast collection of Electronic Health Records. These records, usually referred to simply by their initials, EHR, provide an electronic version of a patient's full medical history, including diagnoses, medications prescribed, medical images such as X-rays, and all other relevant information collected over time, thus constructing a 'virtual patient'—a concept we will look at later in this chapter. As well as using big data to improve patient care and cut costs, by pooling the information generated from a variety of online sources it becomes possible to think in terms of predicting the course of emerging epidemics.

Google Flu Trends

Every year, like many countries, the US experiences an influenza (or flu) epidemic resulting in stretched medical resources and considerable loss of life. Data from past epidemics supplied by the US Center for Disease Control (CDC), the public health monitoring agency, together with big data analytics, provide the driving force behind researchers' efforts to predict the spread of the illness in order to focus services and reduce its impact.

The Google Flu Trends team started working on predicting flu epidemics using search engine data. They were interested in how the course of the annual flu epidemic might be predicted faster than it currently took the CDC to process its own data. In a letter published in the prestigious scientific journal *Nature* in February 2009, the team of six Google software engineers explained what they were doing. If data could be used to accurately predict the course of the annual US flu epidemic then the illness could be contained, saving lives and medical resources. The Google team explored the idea that this could be achieved by collecting and analysing search engine queries relevant to concerns about the flu. Previous attempts to use online data to predict the spread of the flu had either failed or been met with limited success. However, by learning from earlier mistakes in this pioneering research, Google and the CDC hoped to be successful in using big data generated by search engine queries to improve epidemic tracking.

The CDC and its European counterpart, the European Influenza Surveillance Scheme (EISS), collect data from various sources, including physicians, who report on the number of patients they see with flu-like symptoms. By the time this data is collated it is typically about two weeks old and the epidemic has progressed further. Using data collected in real-time from the Internet, the Google/CDC team aimed to improve the accuracy of epidemic predictions and to deliver results within a single day. To do this, data was collected on flu-related search queries varying from individual Internet searches on flu remedies and symptoms to mass data such as phone calls made to medical advice centres. Google was able to tap into a vast amount of search query data that it had accumulated between 2003 and 2008, and by using

IP addresses it was able to identify the geographic location of where search queries had been generated and thus group the data according to State. The CDC data is collected from ten regions, each containing the cumulative data from a group of States (e.g. Region 9 includes Arizona, California, Hawaii, and Nevada), and this was then integrated into the model.

The Google Flu Trends project hinged on the known result that there is a high correlation between the number of flu-related online searches and visits to the doctor's surgery. If a lot of people in a particular area are searching for flu-related information online, it might then be possible to predict the spread of flu cases to adjoining areas. Since the interest is in finding trends, the data can be anonymized and hence no consent from individuals is required. Using their five-year accumulation of data, which they limited to the same time-frame as the CDC data, and so collected only during the flu season, Google counted the weekly occurrence of each of the fifty million most common search queries covering all subjects. These search query counts were then compared with the CDC flu data, and those with the highest correlation were used in the flu trends model. Google chose to use the top forty-five flu-related search terms and subsequently tracked these in the search queries people were making. The complete list of search terms is secret but includes, for example, 'influenza complication', 'cold/flu remedy', and 'general influenza symptoms'. The historical data provided a baseline from which to assess current flu activity on the chosen search terms and by comparing the new real-time data against this, a classification on a scale from 1 to 5, where 5 signified the most severe, was established.

Used in the 2011–12 and 2012–13 US flu seasons, Google's big data algorithm famously failed to deliver. After the flu season ended, its predictions were checked against the CDC's actual data. In building the model, which should be a good representation of flu trends from the data available, the Google Flu Trends algorithm over-predicted the number of flu cases by at least

50 per cent during the years it was used. There were several reasons why the model did not work well. Some search terms were intentionally excluded because they did not fit the expectations of the research team. The much publicized example is that high-school basketball, seemingly unrelated to the flu, was nevertheless highly correlated with the CDC data, but it was excluded from the model. Variable selection, the process by which the most appropriate predictors are chosen, always presents a challenging problem and so is done algorithmically to avoid bias. Google kept the details of their algorithm confidential, noting only that high-school basketball came in the top 100 and justifying its exclusion by pointing out that the flu and basketball both peak at the same time of year.

As we have noted, in constructing their model Google used forty-five search terms as predictors of the flu. Had they only used one, for example 'influenza' or 'flu', important and relevant information such as all the searches on 'cold remedy' would have gone unnoticed and unreported. Accuracy in prediction is improved by having a sufficient number of search terms but it can also decrease if there are too many. Current data is used as training data to construct a model that predicts future data trends, and when there are too many predictors, small random cases in the training data are modelled and so, although the model fits the training data very well, it does not predict well. This seemingly paradoxical phenomenon, called 'over-fitting', was not taken into account sufficiently by the team. Omitting high-school basketball as simply being coincidental to the flu season made sense, but there were fifty million distinct search terms and with such a big number it is almost inevitable that others will correlate strongly with the CDC but not be relevant to flu trends.

Visits to the doctor with flu-like symptoms often resulted in a diagnosis that was not the flu (e.g. it was the common cold). The data Google used, collected selectively from search engine queries, produced results that are not scientifically sound given the obvious bias produced, for example by eliminating everyone who does not use a computer and everyone using other search engines. Another issue that may have led to poor results was that customers searching Google on 'flu symptoms' would probably have explored a number of flu-related websites, resulting in their being counted several times and thus inflating the numbers. In addition, search behaviour changes over time, especially during an epidemic, and this should be taken into account by updating the model regularly. Once errors in prediction start to occur, they tend to cascade, which is what happened with the Google Flu Trends predictions: one week's errors were passed along to the next week. Search queries were considered as they had actually occurred and not grouped according to spelling or phrasing. Google's own example was that 'indications of flu', 'flu indications', and 'indications of the flu' were each counted separately.

The work, which dates back to 2007–8, has been much criticized, sometimes unfairly, but the criticism has usually related to lack of transparency, for example the refusal to reveal all the chosen search terms and unwillingness to respond to requests from the academic community for information. Search engine query data is not the product of a designed statistical experiment and finding a way to meaningfully analyse such data and extract useful knowledge is a new and challenging field that would benefit from collaboration. For the 2012–13 flu season, Google made significant changes to its algorithms and started to use a relatively new mathematical technique called Elasticnet, which provides a rigorous means of selecting and reducing the number of predictors required. In 2011, Google launched a similar program for tracking Dengue fever, but they are no longer publishing predictions and, in 2015, Google Flu Trends was withdrawn. They are, however, now sharing their data with academic researchers.

Google Flu Trends, one of the earlier attempts at using big data for epidemic prediction, provided useful insights to researchers who came after them. Even though the results did not live up to expectations, it seems likely that in the future better techniques will be developed and the full potential of big data in tracking epidemics realized. One such attempt was made by a group of scientists from the Los Alamos National Laboratory in the USA, using data from Wikipedia. The Delphi Research Group at Carnegie Mellon University won the CDC's challenge to 'Predict the Flu' in both 2014–15 and 2015–16 for the most accurate forecasters. The group successfully used data from Google, Twitter, and Wikipedia for monitoring flu outbreaks.

The West Africa Ebola outbreak

The world has experienced many pandemics in the past; the Spanish flu of 1918–19 killed somewhere between twenty million and fifty million people and in total infected about 500 million people. Very little was known about the virus, there was no effective treatment, and the public health response was limited—necessarily so, due to lack of knowledge. This changed in 1948 with the inauguration of the World Health Organization (WHO), charged with monitoring and improving global health through worldwide cooperation and collaboration. On 8 August 2014, at a teleconference meeting of the International Health Regulations Emergency Committee, the WHO announced that an outbreak of the Ebola virus in West Africa formally constituted a 'public health emergency of international concern' (PHEIC). Using a term defined by the WHO, the Ebola outbreak constituted an 'extraordinary event' requiring an international effort of unprecedented proportions in order to contain it and thus avert a pandemic.

The West Africa Ebola outbreak in 2014, primarily confined to Guinea, Sierra Leone, and Liberia, presented a different set of problems to the annual US flu outbreak. Historical data on Ebola was either not available or of little use since an outbreak of these proportions had never been recorded, and so new strategies for dealing with it needed to be developed. Given that knowledge of population movements help public health professionals monitor the spread of epidemics, it was believed that the information held by mobile phone companies could be used to track travel in the infected areas, and measures put in place, such as travel restrictions, that would contain the virus, ultimately saving lives. The resulting real-time model of the outbreak would predict where the next instances of the disease were most likely to occur and resources could be focused accordingly.

The digital information that can be garnered from mobile phones is fairly basic: the phone number of both the caller and the person being called, and an approximate location of the caller—a call made on a mobile phone generates a trail that can be used to estimate the caller's location according to the tower used for each call. Getting access to this data posed a number of problems: privacy issues were a genuine concern as individuals who had not given consent for their calls to be tracked could be identified.

In the West African countries affected by Ebola, mobile phone density was not uniform, with the lowest percentages occurring in poor rural areas. For example, in 2013 just over half the households in Liberia and Sierra Leone, two of the countries directly affected by the outbreak in 2014, had a mobile phone, but even so they could provide sufficient data to usefully track movement.

Some historic mobile phone data was given to the Flowminder Foundation, a non-profit organization based in Sweden, dedicated to working with big data on public health issues that affect the world's poorer countries. In 2008, Flowminder were the first to use mobile operator data to track population movements in a medically challenging environment, as part of an initiative by the WHO to eradicate malaria, so they were an obvious choice to work on the Ebola crisis. A distinguished international team used anonymized historic data to construct maps of population movements in the areas affected by Ebola. This historic data was of limited use since behaviour changes during epidemics, but it does give strong indications of where people will tend to travel, given an emergency. Mobile phone mast activity records provide real-time population activity details.

However, the Ebola prediction figures published by WHO were over 50 per cent higher than the cases actually recorded.

The problems with both the Google Flu Trends and Ebola analyses were similar in that the prediction algorithms used were based only on initial data and did not take into account changing conditions. Essentially, each of these models assumed that the number of cases would continue to grow at the same rate in the future as they had before the medical intervention began. Clearly, medical and public health measures could be expected to have positive effects and these had not been integrated into the model.

The Zika virus, transmitted by Aedes mosquitoes, was first recorded in 1947 in Uganda, and has since spread as far afield as Asia and the Americas. The current Zika virus outbreak, identified in Brazil in 2015, resulted in another PHEIC. Lessons have been learned regarding statistical modelling with big data from work by Google Flu Trends and during the Ebola outbreak, and it is now generally acknowledged that data should be collected from multiple sources. Recall that the Google Flu Trends project collected data only from its own search engine.

The Nepal earthquake

So what is the future for epidemic tracking using big data? The real-time characteristics of mobile phone call detail records (CDRs) have been used to assist in monitoring population movements in disasters as far ranging as the Nepal earthquake and the swine-flu outbreak in Mexico. For example, an international Flowminder team, with scientists from the Universities of Southampton and Oxford, as well as institutions in the US and

China, following the Nepal earthquake of 25 April 2015, used CDRs to provide estimates of population movements. A high percentage of the Nepali population has a mobile phone and by using the anonymized data of twelve million subscribers, the Flowminder team was able to track population movements within nine days of the earthquake. This quick response was due in part to having in place an agreement with the main service provider in Nepal, technical details of which were only completed a week before the disaster. Having a dedicated server with a 20 Tb hard drive in the providers' data centre enabled the team to start work immediately, resulting in information being made available to disaster relief organizations within nine days of the earthquake.

Big data and smart medicine

Every time a patient visits a doctor's office or hospital, electronic data is routinely collected. Electronic health records constitute legal documentation of a patient's healthcare contacts: details such as patient history, medications prescribed, and test results are recorded. Electronic health records may also include sensor data such as Magnetic Resonance Imaging (MRI) scans. The data may be anonymized and pooled for research purposes. It is estimated that in 2015, an average hospital in the USA will store over 600 Tb of data, most of which is unstructured. How can this data be mined to give information that will improve patient care and cut costs? In short, we take the data, both structured and unstructured, identify features relevant to a patient or patients, and use statistical techniques such as classification and regression to model outcomes. Patient notes are primarily in the format of unstructured text, and to effectively analyse these requires natural language processing techniques such as those used by IBM's Watson, which is discussed in the next section.

According to IBM, by 2020 medical data is expected to double every seventy-three days. Increasingly used for monitoring healthy individuals, wearable devices are widely used to count the number of steps we take each day; measure and balance our calorie requirements; track our sleep patterns; as well as giving immediate information on our heart rate and blood pressure. The information gleaned can then be uploaded onto our PCs and records kept privately or, as is sometimes the case, shared voluntarily with employers. This veritable cascade of data on individuals will provide healthcare professionals with valuable public health data as well as providing a means for recognizing changes in individuals that might help avoid, for example, a heart attack. Data on populations will enable physicians to track, for example, side-effects of a particular medication based on patient characteristics.

Following the completion of the Human Genome Project in 2003, genetic data will increasingly become an important part of our individual medical records as well as providing a wealth of research data. The aim of the Human Genome Project was to map all the genes of humans. Collectively, the genetic information of an organism is called its genome. Typically, the human genome contains about 20,000 genes and mapping such a genome requires about 100 Gb of data. Of course, this is a highly complex, specialized, and multi-faceted area of genetic research, but the implications following the use of big data analytics are of interest. The information about genes thus collected is kept in large databases and there has been concern recently that these might be hacked and patients who contributed DNA would be identified. It has been suggested that, for security purposes, false information should be added to the database, although not enough to render it useless for medical research. The interdisciplinary field of bioinformatics has flourished as a consequence of the need to manage and analyse the big data generated by genomics. Gene sequencing has become increasingly rapid and much cheaper in recent years, so that mapping individual genomes is now practical. Taking into account the cost of fifteen years of research, the first human genome sequencing cost nearly US$3 million. Many companies now offer genome sequencing services to individuals at an affordable price.

Growing out of the Human Genome Project, the Virtual Physiological Human (VPH) project aims to build computer representations that will allow clinicians to simulate medical treatments and find the best for a given patient, built on the data from a vast data bank of actual patients. By comparing those with similar symptoms and other medically relevant details, the computer model can predict the likely outcome of a treatment on an individual patient. Data mining techniques are also used and potentially merged with the computer simulations to personalize medical treatment, and so the results of an MRI might integrate with a simulation. The digital patient of the future would contain all the information about a real patient, updated according to smart device data. However, as is increasingly the case, data security is a significant challenge faced by the project.

Watson in medicine

In 2007, IBM decided to build a computer to challenge the top competitors in the US television game show, *Jeopardy*. Watson, a big data analytics system named after the founder of IBM, Thomas J. Watson, was pitted against two *Jeopardy* champions: Brad Rutter, with a winning streak of seventy-four appearances; and Ken Jennings, who had won a staggering total of US$3.25 million. *Jeopardy* is a quiz show in which the host of the show gives an 'answer' and the contestant has to guess the 'question'. There are three contestants and the answers or clues come in several categories such as science, sport, and world history together with less standard, curious categories such as 'before and after'. For example, given the clue 'His tombstone in a Hampshire churchyard reads "knight, patriot, physician and man of letters; 22 May 1859–7 July 1930"', the answer is 'Who is Sir Arthur Conan Doyle?'. In the less obvious category 'catch these men', given the clue 'Wanted for 19 murders, this Bostonian went on the run in 1995 and was finally nabbed in Santa Monica in 2011', the answer is 'Who was Whitey Bulger?'. Clues that were delivered to Watson as text and audio-visual cues were omitted from the competition.

Natural language processing (NLP), as it is known in artificial intelligence (AI), represents a huge challenge to computer science and was crucial to the development of Watson. Information also has to be accessible and retrievable, and this is a problem in machine learning. The research team started out by analysing *Jeopardy* clues according to their lexical answer type (LAT), which classifies the kind of answer specified in the clue. For the second of these examples, the LAT is 'this Bostonian'. For the first example, there is no LAT, the pronoun 'it' does not help. Analysing 20,000 clues the IBM team found 2,500 unique LATs but these covered only about half the clues. Next, the clue is parsed to identify key words and the relationships between them. Relevant documents are retrieved and searched from the computer's structured and unstructured data. Hypotheses are generated based on the initial analyses, and by looking for deeper evidence potential answers are found.

To win *Jeopardy*, fast advanced natural language processing techniques, machine learning, and statistical analysis were crucial. Among other factors to consider were accuracy and choice of category. A baseline for acceptable performance was computed using data from previous winners. After several attempts, deep question and answer analysis, or 'DeepQA', an amalgamation of many AI techniques gave the solution. This system uses a large bank of computers, working in parallel but not connected to the Internet; it is based on probability and the evidence of experts. As well as generating an answer, Watson uses confidence-scoring algorithms to enable the best result to be found. Only when the confidence threshold is reached does Watson indicate that it is ready to give an answer, the equivalent of a human contestant hitting their buzzer. Watson beat the two *Jeopardy* champions.

Jennings, generous in defeat, is quoted as saying, 'I, for one, welcome our new computer overlords'.

The Watson medical system, based on the original *Jeopardy* Watson, retrieves and analyses both structured and unstructured data. Since it builds its own knowledge base it is essentially a system that appears to model human thought processes in a particular domain. Medical diagnoses are based on all available medical knowledge, they are evidence-based, accurate to the extent that the input is accurate and contains all the relevant information, and consistent. Human doctors have experience but are fallible and some are better diagnosticians than others. The process is similar to the Watson of *Jeopardy*, taking into account all the relevant information and returning diagnoses, each with a confidence rating. Watson's built-in AI techniques enable the processing of big data, including the vast amounts generated by medical imaging.

The Watson supercomputer is now a multi-application system and a huge commercial success. In addition Watson has been engaged in humanitarian efforts, for example through a specially developed openware analytics system to assist in tracking the spread of Ebola in Sierra Leone.

Medical big data privacy

Big data evidently has potential to predict the spread of disease and to personalize medicine, but what of the other side of the coin—the privacy of the individual's medical data? Particularly with the growing use of wearable devices and smartphone apps, questions arise as to who owns the data, where it is being stored, who can access and use it, and how secure it is from cyber-attacks. Ethical and legal issues are abundant but not addressed here.

Data from a fitness tracker may become available to an employer and used: favourably, for example to offer bonuses to those who meet certain metrics; or, unfavourably, to determine those who fail to reach the required standards, perhaps leading to an unwanted redundancy offer. In September 2016, a collaborative research team of scientists from the Technische Universität Darmstadt in Germany and the University of Padua in Italy, published the results of their study into fitness tracker data security. Alarmingly, out of the seventeen fitness trackers tested, all from different manufacturers, none was sufficiently secure to stop changes being made to the data and only four took any measures, all bypassed by the team's efforts, to preserve data veracity.

In September 2016 following the Rio Olympic Games, from which most Russian athletes were banned following substantiated reports of a state-run doping programme, medical records of top athletes, including the Williams sisters, Simone Byles, and Chris Froome, were hacked and publicly disclosed by a group of Russian cyber-hackers on the website FancyBears.net. These medical records, held by the World Anti-Doping Agency (WADA) on their data management system ADAMS, revealed only therapeutic use exemptions and therefore no wrong-doing by the cyber-bullied athletes. It is likely that the initial ADAMS hack was the result of spear-phishing email accounts. This technique, whereby an email appears to be sent by a senior trusted source within an organization, such as a healthcare provider, to a more junior member of the same organization, is used to illegally acquire sensitive information such as passwords and account numbers through downloaded malware.

Proofing big data medical databases from cyber-attacks and hence ensuring patient privacy is a growing concern. Anonymized personal medical data is for sale legally but even so it is sometimes possible to identify individual patients. In a valuable exercise highlighting the vulnerability of supposedly secure data, Harvard Data Privacy Lab scientists Latanya Sweeney and Ji Su Yoo, using legally available *encrypted* (i.e. scrambled so that they cannot easily be read; see Chapter 7) medical data originating in

South Korea, were able to decrypt unique identifiers within the records, and identify individual patients through cross-checking with public records.

Medical records are extremely valuable to cyber-criminals. In 2015, the health insurer Anthem declared that its databases had been hacked with over seventy million people affected. Data critical to individual identification, such as name, address, and social security number, was breached by Deep Panda, a Chinese hacking group, using a stolen password to access the system and instal Trojan-horse malware. Critically, the social security numbers, a unique identifier in the USA, were not encrypted, leaving wide open the possibility of identity theft. Many security breaches start with human error: people are busy and do not noticed subtle changes in a Uniform Resource Locator (URL); devices such as flash drives are lost, stolen, and even on occasion deliberately planted, with malware instantly installed once an unsuspecting employee plugs the device into a USB port. Both discontented employees and genuine employee mistakes also account for countless data leaks.

New big data incentives in the management of healthcare are being launched at an increasing rate by world-renowned institutions such as the Mayo Clinic and Johns Hopkins Medical in the USA, the UK's National Health Service (NHS), and Clermont-Ferrand University Hospital in France. Cloud-based systems give authorized users access to data anywhere in the world. To take just one example, the NHS plans to make patient records available via smartphone by 2018. These developments will inevitably generate more attacks on the data they employ, and considerable effort will need to be expended in the development of effective security methods to ensure the safety of that data.

Chapter 6
Big data, big business

In the 1920s, J. Lyons and Co., a British catering firm famous for their 'Corner House' cafés, employed a young Cambridge University mathematician, John Simmons, to do statistical work. In 1947, Raymond Thompson and Oliver Standingford, both of whom had been recruited by Simmons, were sent on a fact-finding visit to the USA. It was on this visit that they first became aware of electronic computers and their potential for executing routine calculations. Simmons, impressed by their findings, sought to persuade Lyons to acquire a computer.

Collaboration with Maurice Wilkes, who was then engaged in building the Electronic Delay Storage Automatic Computer (EDSAC) at the University of Cambridge, resulted in the Lyons Electronic Office. This computer ran on punched cards and was first used by Lyons in 1951 for basic accounting tasks, such as adding up columns of figures. By 1954, Lyons had formed its own computer business and was building the LEO II, followed by the LEO III. Although the first office computers were being installed as early as the 1950s, given their use of valves (6,000 in the case of the LEO I) and magnetic tape, and their very small amount of RAM, these early machines were unreliable and their applications were limited. The original Lyons Electronic Office became widely referred to as the first business computer, paving the way for modern e-commerce and, after several mergers, finally became part of the newly formed International Computers Limited (ICL) in 1968.

e-Commerce

The LEO machines and the massive mainframe computers that followed were suitable only for the number-crunching tasks involved in such tasks as accounting and auditing. Workers who had traditionally spent their days tallying columns of figures now spent their time producing punched cards instead, a task no less tedious while requiring the same high degree of accuracy.

Since the use of computers became feasible for commercial enterprises, there has been interest in how they can be used to improve efficiency, cut costs, and generate profits. The development of the transistor and its use in commercially available computers resulted in ever-smaller machines, and in the early 1970s the first personal computers were being introduced. However, it was not until 1981, when International Business Machines (IBM) launched the IBM-PC on the market, with the use of floppy disks for data storage, that the idea really took off for business. The word-processing and spreadsheet capabilities of succeeding generations of PCs were largely responsible for relieving much of the drudgery of routine office work.

The technology that facilitated electronic data storage on floppy disks soon led to the idea that in future, businesses could be run effectively without the use of paper. In 1975 an article in the American magazine *BusinessWeek* speculated that the almost paper-free office would be a reality by 1990. The suggestion was that by eliminating or significantly reducing the use of paper, an office would become more efficient and costs would be reduced. Paper use in offices declined for a while in the 1980s when much of the paperwork that used to be found in filing cabinets was transferred to computers, but it then rose to an all-time high in 2007, with photocopies accounting for the majority of the increase. Since 2007, paper use has been gradually declining, thanks largely to the increased use of mobile smart devices and facilities such as the electronic signature.

Although the optimistic aspiration of the early digital age to make an office paperless has yet to be fulfilled, the office environment has been revolutionized by email, word-processing, and electronic spreadsheets. But it was the widespread adoption of the Internet that made e-commerce a practical proposition.

Online shopping is perhaps the most familiar example. As customers, we enjoy the convenience of shopping at home and avoiding time-consuming queues. The disadvantages to the customer are few but, depending on the type of transaction, the lack of contact with a store employee may inhibit the use of online purchasing. Increasingly, these problems are being overcome by online customer advice facilities such as 'instant chat', online reviews, and star rankings, a huge choice of goods and services together with generous return policies. As well as buying and paying for goods, we can now pay our bills, do our banking, buy airline tickets, and access a host of other services all online.

eBay works rather differently and is worth mentioning because of the huge amounts of data it generates. With transactions being made through sales and auction bids, eBay generates approximately 50 Tb of data a day, collected from every search, sale, and bid made on their website by a claimed 160 million active users in 190 countries. Using this data and the appropriate analytics they have now implemented recommender systems similar to those of Netflix, discussed later in this chapter.

Social networking sites provide businesses with instant feedback on everything from hotels and vacations to clothes, computers, and yoghurt. By using this information, businesses can see what works, how well it works, and what gives rise to complaints, while fixing problems before they get out of control. Even more valuable is the ability to predict what customers want to buy based on previous sales or website activity. Social networking sites such as Facebook and Twitter collect massive amounts of unstructured data that businesses can benefit from commercially given the appropriate analytics. Travel websites, such as TripAdvisor, also share information with third parties.

Pay-per-click advertising

Professionals are now increasingly acknowledging that appropriate use of big data can provide useful information and generate new customers through improved merchandising and use of better targeted advertising. Whenever we use the Web we are almost inevitably aware of online advertising and we may even post free advertisements ourselves on various bidding sites such as eBay.

One of the most popular kinds of advertising follows the pay-per-click model, which is a system by which relevant advertisements pop up when you are doing an online search. If a business wants their advertisement to be displayed in connection with a particular search term, they place a bid with the service provider on a keyword associated with that search term. They also declare a daily maximum budget. The adverts are displayed in order according to a system based in part on which advertiser has bid the highest for that term.

If you click on their advertisement, the advertiser then must pay the service provider what they bid. Businesses only pay when an interested party clicks on their advertisement, so these adverts must be a good match for the search term to make it more likely that a Web surfer will click on them. Sophisticated algorithms ensure that for the service provider, for example Google or Yahoo, revenue is maximized. The best known implementation of pay-per-click advertising is Google's Adwords. When we search on Google the advertisements that automatically appear on the side of the screen are generated by Adwords. The downside is that clicks can be expensive, and there is also a limit on the number of characters you are allowed to use so that your advertisement will not take up too much space.

Click fraud is also a problem. For example, a rival company may click on your advertisement repeatedly in order to use up your daily budget. Or a malicious computer program, called a clickbot, may be used to generate clicks. The victim of this kind of fraud is the advertiser, since the service provider gets paid and no customers are involved. However, since it is in the best interests of providers to ensure security and so protect a lucrative business, considerable research effort is being made to counteract fraud. Probably the simplest method is to keep track of how many clicks are needed on average to generate a purchase. If this suddenly increases or if there are a large number of clicks and virtually no purchases then fraudulent clicking seems likely.

In contrast to pay-per-click arrangements, targeted advertising is based explicitly on each person's online activity record. To see how this works, we'll start by looking more closely at cookies, which I mentioned briefly in Chapter 1.

Cookies

This term first appeared in 1979 when the operating system UNIX ran a program called Fortune Cookie, which delivered random quotes to the users generated from a large database. Cookies come in several forms, all of which originate externally and are used to keep a record of some activity on a website and/or computer. When you visit a website, a message consisting of a small file that is stored on your computer is sent by a Web server to your browser. This message is one example of a cookie, but there are many other kinds, such as those used for user-authentication purposes and those used for third-party tracking.

Targeted advertising

Every click you make on the Internet is being collected and used for targeted advertising.

This user data is sent to third-party advertising networks and stored on your computer as a cookie. When you click on other sites supported by this network, advertisements for products you looked at previously will be displayed on your screen. Using Lightbeam, a free add-on to Mozilla Firefox, you can keep track of which companies are collecting your Internet activity data.

Recommender systems

Recommender systems provide a filtering mechanism by which information is provided to users based on their interests. Other types of recommender systems, not based on the users' interests, show what other customers are looking at in real-time and often these will appear as 'trending'. Netflix, Amazon, and Facebook are examples of businesses that use these systems.

A popular method for deciding what products to recommend to a customer is *collaborative filtering*. Generally speaking, the algorithm uses data collected on individual customers from their previous purchases and searches, and compares this to a large database of what other customers liked and disliked in order to make suitable recommendations for further purchasing. However, a simple comparison does not generally produce good results. Consider the following example.

Suppose an online bookstore sells a cookery book to a customer. It would be easy to subsequently recommend all cookery books, but this is unlikely to be successful in securing further purchases. There are far too many of them, and the customer already knows he or she likes cookery books. What is needed is a way of reducing

	Daily Salads	Pasta Today	Desserts Tomorrow	Wine For All
Smith	bought		bought	
Jones	bought			bought
Brown		bought	bought	bought

19. **Books bought by Smith, Jones, and Brown.**

the number of books to those that the customer might actually buy. Let's look at three customers, Smith, Jones, and Brown, together with their book purchases (Figure 19).

The question for the recommender system is which book should be recommended to Smith and which recommended to Jones. We want to know if Smith is more likely to buy *Pasta Today* or *Wine for All*.

To do this we need to use a statistic that is often used for comparing sets and is called the *Jaccard index*. This is defined as the number of items the two sets have in common divided by the total number of distinct items in the two sets. The index measures the similarity between the two sets as the proportion they have in common. The Jaccard distance, defined as one minus the Jaccard index, measures the dissimilarity between them.

Looking again at Figure 19, we see that Smith and Jones have one book purchase in common, *Daily Salads*. Between them they have purchased three distinct books, *Daily Salads*, *Desserts Tomorrow*, and *Wine for All*. This gives them a Jaccard index of 1/3 and a Jaccard distance of 2/3. Figure 20 shows the calculation for all the possible pairs of customers.

Smith and Jones have a higher Jaccard index, or similarity score, than Smith and Brown. This means that Smith and Jones are closer in their purchasing habits—so we recommend *Wine for All*

	Number of titles in common	Total number of distinct titles purchased	Jaccard index	Jaccard distance
Smith and Jones	1	3	1/3	2/3
Smith and Brown	1	4	1/4	3/4
Jones and Brown	1	4	1/4	3/4

20. **Jaccard index and distance.**

to Smith. What should we recommend to Jones? Smith and Jones have a higher Jaccard index than Jones and Brown, so we recommend *Desserts Tomorrow* to Jones.

Now suppose that customers rate purchases on a five-star system. To make use of this information we need to find other customers who gave the same rating to particular books and see what else they bought as well as considering their purchasing history. The star ratings for each purchase are given in Figure 21.

In this example a different calculation, called the *cosine similarity measure*, which takes the star ratings into account, is described. For this calculation, the information given in the Star Ratings table is represented as vectors. The length or magnitude of the vectors is normalized to 1 and plays no further part in the calculations. The direction of the vectors is used as a way of finding how similar the two vectors are and so who has the best star rating. Based on the theory of vector spaces, a value for the cosine similarity between

	Daily Salads	Pasta Today	Desserts Tomorrow	Wine For All
Smith	5		3	
Jones	2			5
Brown		1	4	3

21. **Star ratings for purchases.**

the two vectors is found. The calculation is rather different to the familiar trigonometry method, but the basic properties still hold with cosines taking values between 0 and 1. For example, if we find that the cosine similarity between two vectors, each representing a person's star ratings, is 1 then the angle between them is 0 since cosine (0) = 1, and so they must coincide and we can conclude that they have identical tastes. The higher the value of the cosine similarity the greater the similarity in taste.

If you want to see the mathematical details, there are references in the Further reading section at the end of this VSI. What is interesting from our perspective is that the cosine similarity between Smith and Jones works out to be 0.350, and between Smith and Brown it is 0.404. This is a reversal of the previous result, indicating that Smith and Brown have tastes closer than those of Smith and Jones. Informally, this can be interpreted as Smith and Brown being closer in their opinion of *Desserts Tomorrow* than Smith and Jones were in their opinion of *Daily Salads*.

Netflix and Amazon, which we will look at in the next section, both use collaborative filtering algorithms.

Amazon

In 1994, Jeff Bezos founded Cadabra, but soon changed the name to Amazon and in 1995 Amazon.com was launched. Originally an online book store, it is now an international e-commerce company with over 304 million customers worldwide. It produces and sells a diverse range from electronic devices to books and even fresh food items such as yoghurt, milk, and eggs through Amazon Fresh. It is also a leading big data company, with Amazon Web Services providing Cloud-based big data solutions for business, using developments based on Hadoop.

Amazon collected data on what books were bought, what books a customer looked at but did not buy, how long they spent searching, how long they spent looking at a particular book, and whether or not the books they saved were translated into purchases. From this they could determine how much a customer spent on books monthly or annually, and determine whether they were regular customers. In the early days, the data Amazon collected was analysed using standard statistical techniques. Samples were taken of a person and, based on the similarities found, Amazon would offer customers more of the same. Taking this a step further, in 2001 researchers at Amazon applied for and were granted a patent on a technique called item-to-item collaborative filtering. This method finds similar items, not similar customers.

Amazon collects vast amounts of data including addresses, payment information, and details of everything an individual has ever looked at or bought from them. Amazon uses its data in order to encourage the customer to spend more money with them by trying to do as much of the customer's market research as possible. In the case of books, for example, Amazon needs to provide not only a huge selection but to focus recommendations on the individual customer. If you subscribe to Amazon Prime, they also track your movie watching and reading habits. Many customers use smartphones with GPS capability, allowing Amazon to collect data showing time and location. This substantial amount of data is used to construct customer profiles allowing similar individuals and their recommendations to be matched.

Since 2013, Amazon has been selling customer metadata to advertisers in order to promote their Web services operation, resulting in huge growth. For Amazon Web Services, their Cloud computing platform, security is paramount and multi-faceted. Passwords, key-pairs, and digital signatures are just a few of the security techniques in place to ensure that clients' accounts are available only to those with the correct authorization.

Amazon's own data is similarly multi-protected and encrypted, using the AES (Advanced Encryption Standard) algorithm, for storage in dedicated data centres around the world, and Secure Socket Layer (SSL), the industry standard, is used for establishing a secure connection between two machines, such as a link between your home computer and Amazon.com.

Amazon is pioneering *anticipatory shipping* based on big data analytics. The idea is to use big data to anticipate what a customer will order. Initially the idea is to ship a product to a delivery hub before an order actually materializes. As a simple extension, a product can be shipped with a delighted customer receiving a free surprise package. Given Amazon's returns policy, this is not a bad idea. It is anticipated that most customers will keep the items they do order since they are based on their personal preferences, found by using big data analytics. Amazon's 2014 patent on anticipatory shipping also states that goodwill can be bought by sending a promotional gift. Goodwill, increased sales through targeted marketing, and reduced delivery times all make this what Amazon believes to be a worthwhile venture. Amazon also filed for a patent on autonomous flying drone delivery, called Prime Air. In September 2016, the US Federal Aviation Administration relaxed the rules for flying drones by commercial organizations, allowing them, in certain highly controlled situations, to fly beyond the line of sight of the operator. This could be the first stepping stone in Amazon's quest to deliver packages within thirty minutes of an order being placed, perhaps leading to a drone delivery of milk after your smart refrigerator sensor has indicated that you are running out.

Amazon Go, located in Seattle, is a convenience food store and is the first of its kind with no checkout required. As of December 2016 it was only open to Amazon employees and plans for it to be available to the general public in January 2017 have been postponed. At present, the only technical details available are from the patent submitted two years ago, which describes a system eliminating the need to go through an item-by-item checkout. Instead, the details of a customer's actual cart are automatically added to their virtual cart as they shop. Payment is made electronically as they leave the store through a transition area, as long as they have an Amazon account and a smartphone with the Amazon Go app. The Go system is based on a series of sensors, a great many of them, used to identify when an item is taken from or returned to a shelf.

This will generate a huge amount of commercially useful data for Amazon. Clearly, since every shopping action made between entering and leaving the store is logged, Amazon will be able to use this data to make recommendations for your next visit in a way similar to their online recommendation system. However, there may well be issues about how much we value our privacy, especially given aspects such as the possibility mentioned in the patent application of using facial recognition systems to identify customers.

Netflix

Another Silicon Valley company, Netflix, started in 1997 as a postal DVD rental company. You took out a DVD and added another to your queue, and they would then be sent out in turn. Rather usefully, you had the ability to prioritize your queue. This service is still available and still lucrative, though it appears to be gradually winding down. Now an international, Internet streaming, media provider with approximately seventy-five million subscribers across 190 different countries, in 2015 Netflix successfully expanded into providing its own original programmes.

Netflix collects and uses huge amounts of data to improve customer service, such as offering recommendations to individual customers while endeavouring to provide reliable streaming of its movies. Recommendation is at the heart of the Netflix business model and most of its business is driven by the data-based recommendations it is able to offer customers. Netflix now tracks what you watch, what you browse, what you search for, and the day and time you do all these things. It also records whether you are using an iPad, TV, or something else.

In 2006, Netflix announced a crowdsourcing competition aimed at improving their recommender systems. They were offering a $1 million prize for a collaborative filtering algorithm that would improve by 10 per cent the prediction accuracy of user movie ratings. Netflix provided the training data, over 100 million items, for this machine learning and data mining competition—and no other sources could be used. Netflix offered an interim prize (the Progress Prize) worth $50,000, which was won by the Korbell team in 2007 for solving a related but somewhat easier problem. Easier is a relative term here, since their solution combined 107 different algorithms to come up with two final algorithms, which, with ongoing development, are still being used by Netflix. These algorithms were gauged to cope with 100 million ratings as opposed to the five billion that the full prize algorithm would have had to be able to manage. The full prize was eventually awarded in 2009 to the BellKor's Pragmatic Chaos team whose algorithm represented a 10.06 per cent improvement over the existing one. Netflix never fully implemented the winning algorithm, primarily because by this time their business model had changed to the now-familiar one of media streaming.

Once Netflix expanded their business model from a postal service to providing movies by streaming, they were able to gather a lot more information on their customers' preferences and viewing habits, which in turn enabled them to provide improved recommendations. However, in a departure from the digital modality, Netflix employs part-time *taggers*, a total of about forty people worldwide who watch movies and tag the content, labelling them as, for example, 'science fiction' or 'comedy'. This is how films get categorized—using human judgement and not a computer algorithm initially; that comes later.

Netflix uses a wide range of recommender algorithms that together make up a recommender system. All these algorithms act on the aggregated big data collected by the company. Content-based filtering, for example, analyses the data reported by the 'taggers' and finds similar movies and TV programmes according to criteria such as genre and actor. Collaborative filtering monitors such things as your viewing and search habits. Recommendations are based on what viewers with similar profiles watched. This was less successful when a user account has more than one user, typically several members of a family, with inevitably different tastes and viewing habits. In order to overcome this problem, Netflix created the option of multiple profiles within each account.

On-demand Internet TV is another area of growth for Netflix and the use of big data analytics will become increasingly important as they continue to develop their activities. As well as collecting search data and star ratings, Netflix can now keep records on how often users pause or fast forward, and whether or not they finish watching each programme they start. They also monitor how, when, and where they watched the programme, and a host of other variables too numerous to mention. Using big data analytics we are told that they are now even able to predict quite accurately whether a customer will cancel their subscription.

Data science

'Data scientist' is the generic title given to those who work in the field of big data. The McKinsey Report of 2012 highlighted the lack of data scientists in the USA alone, estimating that by 2018 the shortage would reach 190,000. The trend is apparent worldwide and even with government initiatives promoting data science skills training, the gap between available and required expertise seems to be widening. Data science is becoming a popular study option in universities but graduates so far have been unable to meet the demands of commerce and industry, where positions in data science offer high salaries to experienced applicants. Big data for commercial enterprises is concerned with profit, and disillusionment will set in quickly if an over-burdened data analyst with insufficient experience fails to deliver the expected positive results. All too often, firms are asking for a one-size-fits-all model of data scientist who is expected to be competent in everything from statistical analysis to data storage and data security.

Data security is of crucial importance to any firm and big data creates its own security issues. In 2016, the Netflix Prize 2 initiative was cancelled because of data security concerns. Other recent data hacks include Adobe in 2013, eBay and JP Morgan Chase Bank in 2014, Anthem (a US health insurance company) and Carphone Warehouse in 2015, MySpace in 2016, and LinkedIn—a 2012 hack not discovered until 2016. This is a small sample; many more companies have been hacked or suffered other types of security breaches leading to the unauthorized dissemination of sensitive data. In Chapter 7, we will look at some of the big data security breaches in depth.

Chapter 7
Big data security and the Snowden case

In July 2009, Amazon Kindle readers found life imitating art when their copy of Orwell's novel *1984* completely disappeared from their devices. In *1984*, the 'memory hole' is used to incinerate documents that are considered subversive or no longer wanted. Documents permanently disappear and history is rewritten. It could almost have been an unfortunate prank but *1984* and Orwell's *Animal Farm* had actually been removed as the result of a dispute between Amazon and the publisher. Customers were angry, having paid for the e-book and assumed that it was therefore their property. A lawsuit filed by a highschool student and one other person was settled out of court. In the settlement, Amazon stated that they would no longer erase books from people's Kindles, except in certain circumstances, including that '*a judicial or regulatory order requires such deletion or modification*'. Amazon offered customers a refund, gift certificate, or to restore the deleted books. In addition to being unable to sell or to lend our Kindle books, it seems we do not actually own them at all.

Although the Kindle incident was in response to a legal problem and was not intended maliciously, it serves to illustrate how straightforward it is to delete e-documents, and without hard copies, how simple it would be to completely eradicate any text viewed as undesirable or subversive. If you pick up the physical version of this book tomorrow and read it you know with absolute certainty it will be the same as it was today but if you read anything on the Web today, you cannot be certain that it will be the same when you read it tomorrow. There is no absolute certainty on the Web. Since e-documents can be modified and updated without the author's knowledge, they can easily be manipulated. This situation could be extremely damaging in many different situations, such as the possibility of someone tampering with electronic medical records. Even digital signatures, designed to authenticate electronic documents, can be hacked. This highlights some of the problems facing big data systems, such as ensuring they actually work as intended, can be fixed when they break down, and are tamper-proof and accessible only to those with the correct authorization.

Securing a network and the data it holds are the key issues here. A basic measure taken to safeguard networks against unauthorized access is to install a *firewall*, which isolates a network from unauthorized outside access through the Internet. Even if a network is secure from direct attack, for example from viruses and trojans, the data stored on it, particularly if it is unencrypted, can still be compromised. For instance, one such technique, that of phishing, attempts to introduce malicious code, usually by sending an email with an executable file or requesting personal or security data such as passwords. But the main problem facing big data is that of hacking.

The retail store Target was hacked in 2013 leading to the theft of the details of an estimated 110 million customer records, including credit card details of forty million people. It is reported that by the end of November the intruders had successfully pushed their malware to most of Target's point-of-sale machines and were able to collect customer card records from real-time transactions. At that time, Target's security system was being monitored twenty-four hours a day by a team of specialists working in Bangalore. Suspicious activity was flagged and the team contacted the primary security team located in Minneapolis, who unfortunately failed to act on the information. The Home Depot hack, which we will look at next, was even bigger but used similar techniques, leading to a massive data theft.

Home Depot hack

On 8 September 2014, Home Depot, which describes itself as the largest home improvement retailer in the world, announced in a press release that its payment data systems had been hacked. In an update on 18 September 2014, Home Depot reported that the attack had affected approximately fifty-six million debit/credit cards. In other words, fifty-six million debit/credit cards details were stolen. In addition, fifty-three million email addresses were also stolen. In this case, the hackers were able to first steal a vendor's log, giving them easy access to the system—but only to the individual vendor's part of the system. This was accomplished by a successful phishing attempt.

The next step required the hackers to access the extended system. At that time, Home Depot was using Microsoft XP operating system, which contained an inherent flaw that the hackers exploited. The self-checkout system was then targeted since this sub-system was itself clearly identifiable within the entire system. Finally, the hackers infected the 7,500 self-checkout terminals with malware to gain customer information. They used BlackPOS, also known as Kaptoxa, a specific malware for scraping credit/debit card information from infected terminals. For security, payment card information should be encrypted when the card is swiped at a point-of-sales terminal but apparently this feature, point-to-point encryption, had not been implemented and so the details were left open for the hackers to take.

The theft was uncovered when banks started to detect fraudulent activity on accounts that had made other recent purchases at Home Depot—the card details had been sold through Rescator, a cybercrime outlet found on the dark Web. It is interesting that people using cash registers, which also take cards, were not affected by this attack. The reason for this appears to be that in the mainframe computer, cash registers were identified only by numbering and so were not readily identifiable as checkout points by the criminals. If Home Depot had also used simple numbering for its self-checkout terminals, this hacking attempt might have been foiled. Having said that, at the time Kaptoxa was deemed state-of-the-art malware and was virtually undetectable, so given the open access to the system the hackers had obtained, it almost certainly would eventually have been introduced successfully.

The biggest data hack yet

In December 2016, Yahoo! announced that a data breach involving over one billion user accounts had occurred in August 2013. Dubbed the biggest ever cyber theft of personal data, or at least the biggest ever divulged by any company, thieves apparently used forged cookies, which allowed them access to accounts without the need for passwords. This followed the disclosure of an attack on Yahoo! in 2014, when 500 million accounts were compromised. Chillingly, Yahoo! alleged the 2014 hack was perpetrated by an unnamed 'state-sponsored actor'.

Cloud security

The list of big data security breaches increases almost daily. Data theft, data ransom, and data sabotage are major concerns in a data-centric world. There have been many scares regarding the security and ownership of personal digital data. Before the digital age we used to keep photos in albums and negatives were our backup. After that, we stored our photos electronically on a hard-drive in our computer. This could possibly fail and we were wise to have back-ups but at least the files were not publicly accessible. Many of us now store data in the Cloud. Photos, videos, home movies all require a lot of storage space and so the Cloud makes sense from that perspective. When you store your files in the Cloud, you are uploading them to a data centre—more likely, they will be distributed across several centres—and more than one copy will be kept.

If you store all your photos in the Cloud, it's highly unlikely with today's sophisticated systems that you would lose them. On the other hand, if you want to delete something, maybe a photo or video, it becomes difficult to ensure all copies have been deleted. Essentially you have to rely on your provider to do this. Another important issue is controlling who has access to the photos and other data you have uploaded to the Cloud. If we want to make big data secure, encryption is vital.

Encryption

Encryption, as mentioned briefly in Chapter 5, refers to methods used to scramble files so that they cannot easily be read, and the basic technique goes back at least as far as Roman times. Suetonius, in his *The Twelve Caesars*, describes how Julius Caesar encoded documents using a three-letter shift to the left. Using this method the word 'secret' would be encoded as 'pbzobq'. Known as a 'Caesar cipher' this is not difficult to break, but even the most secure ciphers used today apply shifting as part of the algorithm.

In 1997, the best publicly available encryption method, Data Encryption Standard (DES), was shown to be breakable, largely due to the increase in computing power available and the relatively short 56-bit key length. Although this provides a possible 2^{56} different key choices, it was possible to decrypt a message by testing each one until the correct key was found. This was done in 1998, in just over twenty-two hours using Deep Crack, a computer built by Electronic Frontier Foundation expressly for this purpose.

In 1997, the National Institute of Standards and Technology (NIST) in the USA, concerned that DES lacked the security needed for protecting top secret documents, launched an open, worldwide competition to find a better encryption method than DES. The competition ended in 2001 with the AES algorithm being chosen. It was submitted as the Rijndael algorithm, combining the names of its two Belgian originators, Joan Daemen and Vincent Rijmen.

AES is a software algorithm used for text encryption with a choice of a 128-, 192-, or 256-bit key length. For the 128-bit key length, the algorithm requires nine processing rounds, each consisting of four steps, plus a final round with only three steps. The AES encryption algorithm is iterative and performs a large number of computations on matrices—just the kind of calculations that are best performed by computers. However, we can describe the process informally without reference to the mathematical transformations.

AES starts by applying a key to the text we want to encrypt. We would no longer be able to recognize the text but given the key, we could easily decode it so more steps are needed. The next step involves substituting each letter with another letter, using a special look-up table, called a Rijndael S-Box. Again, if we have the Rijndael S-Box, we can work backwards to decrypt the message. A Caesar Cipher, where letters are shifted to the left, and a final permutation completes one round. The result is then used to start another round, using a different key and so on, until all rounds have been completed. Of course, we have to be able to decrypt, and for this algorithm the method is reversible.

For the 192-bit key length there are twelve rounds in total. For even greater security, a longer key length, AES 256, can be employed, but most users, including Google and Amazon, find AES 128 sufficient for their big data security needs. AES is secure and has yet to be broken, leading to several governments to ask major companies such as Apple and Google to provide back doors into the encrypted material.

Email security

It has been estimated that in 2015 over 200 billion emails were sent every day, with less than 10 per cent of these being authentic and not spam or with malicious intent. Most emails are not encrypted, making their contents vulnerable to interception by hackers. When I send an unencrypted email, let's say from California to the UK for example, it is divided into data 'packets' and transmitted through a mail server, which is connected to the Internet. The Internet is essentially made up of a big worldwide network of wires, above ground, below ground, and below oceans, plus cell phone towers and satellites. The only continent unconnected by transoceanic cables is Antarctica.

So although the Internet and Cloud-based computing are generally thought of as wireless, they are anything but; data is transmitted through fibre-optic cables laid under the oceans. Nearly all digital communication between continents is transmitted in this way. My email will be sent via transatlantic fibre-optic cables, even if I am using a Cloud computing service. The Cloud, an attractive buzz word, conjures up images of satellites sending data across the world, but in reality Cloud services are firmly rooted in a distributed network of data centres providing Internet access, largely through cables.

Fibre-optic cables provide the fastest means of data transmission and so are generally preferable to satellites. The current extensive research into fibre-optic technology is resulting in ever faster data transmission rates. Transatlantic cables have been the target of some curious and unexpected attacks, including those from sharks intent on biting through the cables. While, according to the International Cable Protection Committee, shark attacks account for fewer than 1 per cent of the faults logged, even so, cables in vulnerable areas are now often protected using Kevlar. Assuming there are no problems with transatlantic cables due to inquisitive sharks, hostile governments, or careless fishermen, and my email makes landfall in the UK and continues on its way, it may be at this point that, as with other Internet data, it is intercepted. In June 2013, Edward Snowden leaked documents revealing that the Government Communications Headquarters (GCHQ) in the UK were tapping into a vast amount of data, received through approximately 200 transatlantic cables, using a system called Tempora.

The Snowden case

Edward Snowden is an American computer professional who was charged with espionage in 2013 after leaking classified information from the US National Security Agency (NSA). This high-profile case brought government mass surveillance capabilities to the attention of the general public, and widespread concerns were expressed regarding individual privacy. Awards made to Snowden since taking this action have been many and include election as rector of the University of Glasgow, the *Guardian*'s Person of the Year 2013, and Nobel Peace Prize nominations in 2014, 2015, and 2016. He has the support of Amnesty International as a whistleblower who provided a service to his country. However, US government officials and politicians have begged to differ in this view.

In June 2013, the *Guardian* newspaper in the UK reported that the NSA was collecting metadata from some of the major US phone networks. This report was swiftly followed by the revelation that a program called PRISM was being used to collect and store Internet data on foreign nationals communicating with the US. A whole slew of electronic leaks followed, incriminating both the US and the UK. A Booz Allen Hamilton employee and NSA contractor working at the Hawaii Cryptologic Center, Edward Snowden, was the source of these leaks, which he sent to members of the media he felt could be trusted not to publish without careful consideration. Snowden's motivations, and the legal issues involved, are beyond the scope of this book but it is apparent that he believed that what had started out as legitimate spying on other countries had now turned in on itself and the NSA was now spying, illegally, on all US citizens.

The free Web scraping tools, DownThemAll, an available extension of Mozilla Firefox, and the program *wget*, give the means to quickly download the entire contents of a website or other Web-related data. These applications, available to authorized users on NSA classified networks, were used by Snowden to download and copy massive amounts of information. He also transferred large amounts of highly sensitive data from one computer system to another. In order to do this, he needed usernames and passwords, which a systems administrator would routinely have. He thus had easy access to many of the classified documents he stole, but not all. To get access to higher than top-secret documents, he had to use the authentication details of higher level user accounts, which security protocols should have prevented. However, since he had created these accounts and had system administrator privileges, he knew the account details. Snowden also managed to persuade at least one NSA employee with security clearance higher than his to tell him their password.

Ultimately, Snowden copied an estimated 1.5 million highly classified documents, of which about 200,000 (Snowden understood that not all of his stolen documents should be made public and was cautious about which should be published) were handed over to trusted reporters, although relatively few of even these were eventually published.

While the details have never been fully revealed by Snowden, it seems he was able to copy the data onto flash drives, which he apparently had no difficulty in taking with him when he left work for the day. Security measures to prevent Snowden from being able to remove these documents were clearly inadequate. Even a simple body scan on exiting the facility would have detected any portable devices, and video surveillance in the offices could also have flagged suspicious activity. In December 2016, the US House of Representatives declassified a document dated September 2016, which remains heavily redacted, reviewing Snowden the man as well as the nature and impact of the leaked documents. From this document it is clear that the NSA had not applied sufficient security measures and as a result the Secure the Net initiative has since been put into operation, although it is yet to be fully implemented.

Snowden had extensive system administrator privileges, but given the extremely sensitive nature of the data, allowing one person to have full access with no safeguards was not acceptable. For example, requiring validation credentials of two people when data was accessed or transferred might have been sufficient to prevent Snowden from illicitly copying files. It is also curious that Snowden could apparently plug in a USB drive and copy anything he wanted. A very simple security measure is to disable DVD and USB ports or not have them installed in the first place. Add further authentication using retina scan to the requirement for a password and it would have been very difficult for Snowden even to access those higher level documents. Modern security techniques are sophisticated and difficult to penetrate if used correctly.

In late 2016, entering 'Edward Snowden' in Google search gave over twenty-seven million results in just over one second; and the search term 'Snowden' gave forty-five million results. Since many of these sites give access to or even display the leaked documents labelled 'Top Secret', they are now firmly in the global public domain and will no doubt remain so. Edward Snowden is currently living in Russia.

In contrast with Edward Snowden's case, WikiLeaks presents a very different story.

WikiLeaks

WikiLeaks is a huge online whistleblowing organization whose aim is to disseminate secret documents. It is funded by donations and staffed largely by volunteers, though it does appear to employ a few people too. As of December 2015, WikiLeaks claims to have published (or leaked) more than ten million documents. WikiLeaks maintains its highly public profile through its own website, Twitter, and Facebook.

Highly controversial, WikiLeaks and its leader Julian Assange hit the headlines on 22 October 2010 when a vast amount of classified data—391,832 documents—dubbed 'Iraq War Logs' was made public. This followed the approximately 75,000 documents constituting 'The Afghan War Diary' that had already been leaked on 25 July 2010.

An American army soldier, Bradley Manning, was responsible for both leaks. Working as an intelligence analyst in Iraq, he took a compact disc to work with him and copied secret documents from a supposedly secure personal computer. For this, Bradley Manning, now known as Chelsea Manning, was sentenced in 2013 to thirty-five years in prison following conviction, by court-martial, for violations of the Espionage Act and other related offences. Former US president Barack Obama commuted Chelsea Manning's sentence in January 2017, prior to his leaving office. Ms Manning, who received treatment for gender dysphoria while in prison, was released on 17 May 2017.

Heavily criticized by politicians and governments, WikiLeaks has nonetheless been applauded by and received awards from the likes of Amnesty International (2009) and the UK's *The Economist* (2008), among a long list of others. According to their website, Julian Assange has been nominated for the Nobel Peace Prize in six consecutive years, 2010–15. The Nobel

Committee does not release the names of nominees until fifty years have passed but nominators, who have to meet the strict criteria of the Peace Prize committee, often do publicly announce the names of their nominees. For example, in 2011, Julian Assange was nominated by Snorre Valen, a Norwegian parliamentarian, in support of WikiLeaks exposing alleged human rights violations. In 2015, Assange had the support of former UK member of parliament George Galloway, and in early 2016 a supportive group of academics also called for Assange to be awarded the prize.

Yet by the end of 2016, the tide was turning against Assange and WikiLeaks, at least in part because of alleged bias in their reporting. Against WikiLeaks are ethical concerns regarding the safety and privacy of individuals; corporate privacy; government secrecy; the protection of local sources in areas of conflict; and the public interest in general. The waters are becoming increasingly muddied for Julian Assange and WikiLeaks. For example, in 2016, emails were leaked at a time best suited to damage Hillary Clinton's presidential candidacy, raising questions about WikiLeaks' objectivity, and prompting considerable criticism from a number of well-respected sources.

Regardless of whether you support or condemn the activities of Julian Assange and WikiLeaks, and almost inevitably people will do both, varying with the issue at stake, one of the big technical questions is whether it is possible to shut down WikiLeaks. Since it maintains its data on many servers across the world, some of it in sympathetic countries, it is unlikely that it could be completely shut down, even assuming that this was desirable. However, for increased protection against retaliation following each disclosure, WikiLeaks has issued an insurance file. The unspoken suggestion is that if anything happens to Assange or if WikiLeaks is shut down, the insurance file key will be publicly broadcast. The most recent WikiLeaks insurance file uses AES with a 256-bit key and so it is highly unlikely to be broken.

As of 2016, Edward Snowden is at odds with WikiLeaks. The disagreement comes down to how each of them managed their data leaks. Snowden handed his files over to trusted journalists, who carefully chose which documents to leak. US government officials were informed in advance, and, following their advice, further documents were withheld because of national security concerns. To this day, many have never been disclosed. WikiLeaks appears simply to publish its data with little effort to protect personal information. It still seeks to gather information from whistleblowers, but it is not clear how reliable recent data leaks have been, or indeed whether its selection of the information it presents allows it to be completely disinterested. On its website, WikiLeaks gives instruction for how to use a facility called TOR (The Onion Router) to send data anonymously and ensure privacy, but you do not have to be a whistleblower to use TOR.

TOR and the dark Web

Janet Vertesi, an assistant professor in the Sociology Department at Princeton University, decided to conduct a personal experiment to see if she could keep her pregnancy a secret from online marketers and so prevent her personal information becoming part of the big data pool. In an article published in *TIME* magazine in May 2014, Dr Vertesi gives an account of her experience. She took exceptional privacy measures, including avoiding social media; she downloaded TOR and used it to order many baby-related items; and in-store purchases were paid for in cash. Everything she did was perfectly legal but ultimately she concluded that opting out was costly and time-consuming and made her look, in her own words, like a 'bad citizen'. However, TOR is worth looking at, not least because it made Dr Vertesi feel safe and maintained her privacy from trackers.

TOR is an encrypted network of servers that was originally developed by the US Navy to provide a way of using the

Internet anonymously, and so prevent tracking and the collection of personal data. TOR is an ongoing project, aimed at developing and improving open-source online anonymity environments that anyone concerned about privacy can use. TOR works by encrypting your data, including the sending address, and then anonymizes it by removing part of the header, crucially including the IP address, since an individual can easily be found by back-tracking given that information. The resulting data package is routed through a system of servers or relays, hosted by volunteers, before arriving at its final destination.

On the positive side, users include the military who originally designed it; investigative journalists wishing to protect their sources and information; and everyday citizens wishing to protect their privacy. Businesses use TOR to keep secrets from other businesses; and governments use it to protect sources of sensitive information as well as the information itself. A TOR Project press release gives a list of some of the news items involving TOR between 1999 and 2016.

On the negative side, the TOR anonymity network has been widely used by cyber criminals. Websites are accessible through TOR-hidden services and have the suffix '.onion'. Many of these are extremely unpleasant, including illegal dark websites used for drug dealing, pornography, and money laundering. For example, the highly publicized website Silk Road, part of the dark Web and a supplier of illegal drugs, was accessed through TOR, making it difficult for law enforcement to track it. A major court case followed the arrest of Ross William Ulbricht, who was subsequently convicted of creating and running Silk Road, using the pseudonym Dread Pirate Roberts. The website was closed down but later sprang back up again, and in 2016 was in its third reincarnation under the name Silk Road 3.0.

Deep Web

The deep Web refers to all those websites that cannot be indexed by the usual search engines, such as Google, Bing, and Yahoo! It comprises legitimate sites as well as those that make up the dark Web. It is popularly estimated to be vastly bigger than the familiar surface Web, though even with special deep Web search engines it is difficult to estimate the size of this hidden world of big data.

Chapter 8
Big data and society

Robots and jobs

The eminent economist, John Maynard Keynes, writing during
the British economic depression in 1930, speculated on what
working life would be like a century later. The industrial revolution
had created new city-based jobs in factories and transformed what
had been a largely agrarian society. It was thought that labour-
intensive work would eventually be performed by machines,
leading to unemployment for some and a much-reduced working
week for others. Keynes was particularly concerned with how
people would use their increased leisure time, freed from the
exigencies of gainful employment by technological advances.
Perhaps more pressing was the question of financial support
leading to the suggestion that a universal basic income would
provide a way of coping with the decline in available jobs.

Gradually over the 20th century we have seen jobs in industry
eroded by ever-more sophisticated machines, and although, for
example, many production lines were automated decades ago, the
Keynesian fifteen-hour working week has yet to materialize and
seems unlikely to do so in the near future. The digital revolution
will inevitably change employment, just as the industrial
revolution did, but in ways we are unlikely to be able to predict
accurately. As the technology of the 'Internet of Things' advances,

our world continues to become more data-driven. Using the results of real-time big data analysis to inform decisions and actions will play an increasingly important role in our society.

There are suggestions that people will be needed to build and code machines, but this is speculative and, in any case, is just one area of specialized work where we can realistically expect to see robots increasingly taking the place of people. For example, sophisticated robotic medical diagnosis would reduce the medical workforce. Robotic surgeons, with extended Watson-like capabilities, are likely. Natural language processing, another big data area, will develop to the point where we cannot tell whether we are talking to a robotic device or a doctor—at least, when we are not face-to-face.

However, predicting what jobs humans will be doing once robots have taken over many of the existing roles is difficult. Creativity is supposedly the realm of humans, but computer scientists, working in collaboration at the Universities of Cambridge and Aberystwyth, have developed Adam, a robot scientist. Adam has successfully formulated and tested new hypotheses in the field of genomics, leading to new scientific discoveries. The research has progressed with a team at the University of Manchester successfully developing Eve, a robot that works on drug design for tropical diseases. Both these projects implemented artificial intelligence techniques.

The craft of the novelist appears to be uniquely human, relying on experience, emotion, and imagination, but even this area of creativity is being challenged by robots. The Nikkei Hoshi Shinichi Literary Award accepts novels written or co-written by non-human authors. In 2016, four novels written jointly by people and computers passed the first stage of the competition, without the judges knowing the details regarding authorship.

Although scientists and novelists may eventually work collaboratively with robots, for most of us the impact of our big data driven environment will be more apparent in our daily activities, through smart devices.

Smart vehicles

On 7 December 2016, Amazon announced that it had made its first commercial drone delivery using GPS (global positioning system) to find its way. The recipient, a man living in the countryside near Cambridge in the UK, received a package weighing 4.7 pounds. Drone deliveries can currently be made to only two Amazon Prime Air customers, both living within 5.2 square miles of the fulfilment centre near Cambridge. A video, referenced in the Further reading section, shows the flight. This seems likely to signal the start of big data collection for this program.

Amazon is not the first to make a successful commercial drone delivery. In November 2016, Flirtey Inc. started a drone delivery pizza service in a small area from their home base in New Zealand and there have been similar projects elsewhere. At present, it seems likely that drone delivery services will grow, particularly in remote areas where it might be possible to manage safety issues. Of course, a cyber-attack or simply a breakdown in the computer systems could create havoc: if, for example, a small delivery drone were to malfunction, it could cause injury or death to humans or animals, as well as considerable damage to property.

This is what happened when the software controlling a car travelling along the road at 70 mph was taken over remotely. In 2015, two security experts, Charlie Miller and Chris Valasek, working for *Wired* magazine, demonstrated on a willing victim that Uconnect, a dashboard computer used to connect a vehicle to the Internet, could be hacked remotely while the vehicle was in motion. The report makes alarming reading; the two expert hackers were able to use a laptop Internet connection to control the steering, brakes, and transmission along with other less critical functions such as the air-conditioning and radio of a Jeep Cherokee. The Jeep was travelling at 70 mph on a busy public road when suddenly all response to the accelerator failed, causing considerable alarm to the driver.

As a result of this test, the car manufacturer Chrysler issued a warning to the owners of 1.4 million vehicles and sent out USB drives containing software updates to be installed through a port on the dashboard. The attack was made because of a vulnerability in the smartphone network that was subsequently fixed, but the story serves to illustrate the point that the potential for cyber-attacks on smart vehicles will need to be addressed before the technology becomes fully public.

The advent of autonomous vehicles, from cars to planes, seems inevitable. Planes can already fly themselves, including taking off and landing. Although it's a step away to think of drones being in widespread use for transporting human passengers, they are currently used in farming for intelligent crop spraying and also for military purposes. Smart vehicles are still in the early stages of development for general use but smart devices are already part of the modern home.

Smart homes

As mentioned in Chapter 3, the term 'Internet of Things' (IoT) is a convenient way of referring to the vast numbers of electronic sensors connected to the Internet. For example, any electronic device that can be installed in a home and managed remotely—through a user interface displayed on the resident's television screen, smartphone, or laptop—is a smart device and so part of the IoT. Voice-activated central control points are installed in many homes that manage lighting, heating, garage doors, and many other household devices. Wi-Fi (which stands for 'wireless fidelity', or the capacity to connect with a network, like the Internet, using radio waves rather than wires) connectivity means that you can ask your smart speaker (by its name, which you will have given it) for the local weather or national news reports.

These devices provide Cloud-based services, and are not without their drawbacks when it comes to privacy. As long as the device is switched on, everything you say is recorded and stored in a remote server. In a recent murder investigation, police in the United States asked Amazon to release data from an Echo device (which is voice controlled and connects to the Alexa Voice Service to play music, provide information, news reports, etc.) that they believed would assist them in their inquiries. Amazon was initially unwilling to do so, but the suspect has recently given his permission for them to release the recordings, hoping that they will help prove his innocence.

Further developments, based on Cloud computing, mean that electrical appliances such as washing machines, refrigerators, and home-cleaning robots will be part of the smart home and managed remotely through smartphones, laptops, or home speakers. Since all these systems are Internet controlled they are potentially at risk from hackers, and so security is a big area of research.

Even children's toys are not immune. Named '2014 Innovative Toy of the Year' by the London Toy Industry Association, a smart doll called 'My Friend Cayla' was subsequently hacked. Through an unsecured bluetooth device hidden in the doll, a child can ask the doll questions and hear replies. The German Federal Network Agency, responsible for monitoring Internet communications, has encouraged parents to destroy the doll, which has now been banned, because of the threat to privacy that it presents. Hackers have been able to show that it is fairly easy listen to a child and provide inappropriate answers, including words from the manufacturer's banned list.

Smart cities

Although the smart home is only just becoming a reality, the IoT together with multiple information and communication technologies (ICTs) are now predicted to make smart cities a reality. Many countries, including India, Ireland, the UK, South Korea, China, and Singapore, are already planning smart cities. The idea is that of greater efficiency in a crowded world since cities are growing rapidly. The rural population is moving to the city at an ever-increasing rate. In 2014, about 54 per cent lived in cities and by 2050 the United Nations predicts that about 66 per cent of the world's population will be city dwellers.

The technology of smart cities is propelled by the separate but accumulating ideas from early implementations of the IoT and big data management techniques. For example, driverless cars, remote health monitoring, the smart home, and tele-commuting would all be features of a smart city. Such a city would depend on the management and analysis of the big data accumulated from the sum total of the city's vast sensor array. Big data and the IoT working together are the key to smart cities.

For the community as a whole, one of the benefits would be a smart energy system. This would regulate street lighting, monitor traffic, and even track garbage. All this could be achieved by installing a huge array of radio-frequency identification (RFID) tags and wireless sensors across the city. These tags, which consist of a microchip and a tiny antenna, would send data from individual devices to a central location for analysis. For example, the city governance would monitor traffic by installing RFID tags on vehicles and digital cameras on streets. Improved personal safety would also be a consideration, for example, children could be discretely tagged and monitored through their parents' cell phones. These sensors would create a huge amount of data which would need to be monitored and analysed in real-time, through a central data processing unit. It could then be used for a variety of purposes including gauging traffic flow, identifying congestion, and recommending alternative routes. Data security would clearly be of paramount importance in this context, as any major breakdown in the system or hacking would quickly affect public confidence.

Songdo International Business District in South Korea, scheduled for completion in 2020, has been purpose built as a smart city. One of the main features is that the entire city has fibre-optic broadband. This state-of-the-art technology is used to ensure the desired features of a smart city can be accessed quickly. New smart cities are also being designed to minimize negative environmental effects, making them the sustainable cities of the future. While many smart cities have been planned and, like Songdo, are being purpose built, existing cities will need to modernize their infrastructures gradually.

In May 2016, the United Nations Global Pulse, an initiative aimed at promoting big data research for global benefit, unveiled its open 'Big Ideas Competition 2016: Sustainable Cities' for the ten member states of the Association of Southeast Asian Nations (ASEAN) and the Republic of Korea. By the June deadline, over 250 proposals had been received and the winners in various categories were announced in August 2016. The Grand Prize went to the Republic of Korea for their proposal to improve public transport by reducing waiting times by utilizing crowd-sourcing information on queues.

Looking forward

In this *Very Short Introduction*, we have seen how the science of data has undergone a radical transformation over the past few decades due to the technological advances brought about by the development of the Internet and the digital universe. In this final chapter, we have glimpsed some of the ways our lives may be shaped by big data in the future. While we can't hope to cover in a short introduction all the areas in which big data is making an impact, we have seen some of the diverse applications that already affect us.

The data generated by the world is only going to get bigger. Methods for dealing with all this data effectively and meaningfully will undoubtedly continue to be the subject of intense research, particularly in the area of real-time analysis. The big data revolution marks a sea-change in the way the world works, and as with all technological developments, individuals, scientists, and governments together have a moral responsibility to ensure its proper use. Big data is power. Its potential for good is enormous. How we prevent its abuse is up to us.

Byte size chart

Term	Meaning
Bit	1 binary digit: 0 or 1
Byte	8 bits
Kilobyte (Kb)	1,000 bytes
Megabyte (Mb)	1,000 kilobytes
Gigabyte (Gb)	1,000 megabytes
Terabyte (Tb)	1,000 gigabytes
Petabyte (Pb)	1,000 terabytes
Exabyte (Eb)	1,000 petabytes
Zettabyte (Zb)	1,000 exabytes
Yottabyte (Yb)	1,000 zettabytes

ASCII table for lower case letters

Decimal	Binary	Hex	Letter
97	01100001	61	a
98	01100010	62	b
99	01100011	63	c
100	01100100	64	d
101	01100101	65	e
102	01100110	66	f
103	01100111	67	g
104	01101000	68	h
105	01101001	69	i
106	01101010	6A	j
107	01101011	6B	k
108	01101100	6C	l
109	01101101	6D	m
110	01101110	6E	n
111	01101111	6F	o

Decimal	Binary	Hex	Letter
112	01110000	70	p
113	01110001	71	q
114	01110010	72	r
115	01110011	73	s
116	01110100	74	t
117	01110101	75	u
118	01110110	76	v
119	01110111	77	w
120	01111000	78	x
121	01111001	79	y
122	01111010	7A	z
32	00010000	20	space

Further reading

Chapter 1: The data explosion

David J. Hand, *Information Generation: How Data Rule Our World* (Oneworld, 2007).

Jeffrey Quilter and Gary Urton (eds), *Narrative Threads: Accounting and Recounting in Andean Khipu* (University of Texas Press, 2002).

David Salsburg, *The Lady Tasting Tea: How Statistics Revolutionized Science in the Twentieth Century* (W.H. Freeman and Company, 2001).

Thucydides, *History of the Peloponnesian War*, ed. and intro. M. I. Finley, trans. Rex Warner (Penguin Classics, 1954).

Chapter 2: Why is big data special?

Joan Fisher Box, *R. A. Fisher: The Life of a Scientist* (Wiley, 1978).

David J. Hand, *Statistics: A Very Short Introduction* (Oxford University Press, 2008).

Viktor Mayer-Schönberger and Kenneth Cukier, *Big Data: A Revolution That Will Transform How We Live, Work, and Think* (Mariner Books, 2014).

Chapter 3: Storing big data

C. J. Date, *An Introduction to Database Systems* (8th edn; Pearson, 2003).

Guy Harrison, *Next Generation Databases: NoSQL and Big Data* (Springer, 2015).

Chapter 4: Big data analytics

Thomas S. Kuhn and Ian Hacking, *The Structure of Scientific Revolutions: 50th Anniversary Edition* (University of Chicago Press, 2012).

Bernard Marr, *Big Data: Using SMART Big Data, Analytics and Metrics to Make Better Decisions and Improve Performance* (Wiley, 2015).

Lars Nielson and Noreen Burlingame, *A Simple Introduction to Data Science* (New Street Communications, 2012).

Chapter 5: Big data and medicine

Dorothy H. Crawford, *Ebola: Profile of a Killer Virus* (Oxford University Press, 2016).

N. Generous, G. Fairchild, A. Deshpande, S. Y. Del Valle, and R. Priedhorsky, 'Global Disease Monitoring and Forecasting with Wikipedia', *PLoS Comput Biol* 10(11) (2014), e1003892. doi: 10.1371/journal.pcbi.1003892

Peter K. Ghavami, 'Clinical Intelligence: The Big Data Analytics Revolution in Healthcare. A Framework for Clinical and Business Intelligence' (PhD thesis, 2014).

D. Lazer and R. Kennedy, 'The Parable of Google Flu: Traps in Big Data Analysis', *Science* 343 (2014), 1203–5. <http://scholar.harvard.edu/files/gking/files/0314policyforumff.pdf>.

Katherine Marconi and Harold Lehmann (eds), *Big Data and Health Analytics* (CRC Press, 2014).

Robin Wilson, Elizabeth zu Erbach-Schoenberg, Maximilian Albert, Daniel Power et al., 'Rapid and Near Real-Time Assessments of Population Displacement Using Mobile Phone Data Following Disasters: The 2015 Nepal Earthquake', *PLOS Currents Disasters*, Edition 1, 24 Feb 2016, Research Article. doi: 10.1371/currents.dis.d073fbece328e4c39087bc086d694b5c <http://currents.plos.org/disasters/article/rapid-and-near-real-time-assessments-of-population-displacement-using-mobile-phone-data-following-disasters-the-2015-nepal-earthquake/>.

Chapter 6: Big data, big business

Leo Computers Society, *LEO Remembered, By the People Who Worked on the World's First Business Computers* (Leo Computers Society, 2016).

James Marcus, *Amazonia* (The New Press, 2004).

Bernard Marr, *Big Data in Practice* (Wiley, 2016).

Frank Pasquale, *The Black Box Society: The Secret Algorithms That Control Money and Information* (Harvard University Press, 2015).

Foster Provost and Tom Fawcett, *Data Science for Business* (O'Reilly, 2013).

Chapter 7: Big data security and the Snowden case

Andy Greenberg, *This Machine Kills Secrets* (PLUME, 2013).

Glenn Greenwald, *No Place to Hide: Edward Snowden, the NSA, and the U.S. Surveillance State* (Metropolitan Books, 2014).

Luke Harding, *The Snowden Files* (Vintage Books, 2014).

G. Linden, B. Smith, and J. York, 'Amazon.com Recommendations: Item-to-item Collaborative Filtering', *Internet Computing* 7(1) (2003), 76–80.

Fred Piper and Sean Murphy, *Cryptography: A Very Short Introduction* (Oxford University Press, 2002).

P. W. Singer and Allan Friedman, *Cybersecurity and Cyberwar: What Everyone Needs to Know* (Oxford University Press, 2014).

Nicole Starosielski, *The Undersea Network* (Duke University Press, 2015).

Janet Vertesi, 'How Evasion Matters: Implications from Surfacing Data Tracking Online', *Interface: A Special Topics Journal* 1(1) (2015), Article 13. http://dx.doi.org/10.7710/2373-4914.1013 <http://commons.pacificu.edu/cgi/viewcontent.cgi?article=1013& context=interface>.

Chapter 8: Big data and society

Anno Bunnik and Anthony Cawley, *Big Data Challenges: Society, Security, Innovation and Ethics* (Palgrave Macmillan, 2016).

Samuel Greengard, *The Internet of Things* (MIT Press, 2015).

Robin Hanson, *The Age of Em* (Oxford University Press, 2016).

Websites

<https://www.infoq.com/articles/cap-twelve-years-later-how-the-rules-have-changed>

<https://www.emc.com/collateral/analyst-reports/idc-the-digital-universe-in-2020.pdf>

<http://newsroom.ucla.edu/releases/ucla-research-team-invents-new-249693>
<http://www.ascii-code.com/>
<http://www.tylervigen.com/spurious-correlations>
<https://www.statista.com/topics/846/amazon/>
<https://www.wired.com/2015/07/jeep-hack-chrysler-recalls-1-4m-vehicles-bug-fix/>
<http://www.unglobalpulse.org/about-new>
<https://intelligence.house.gov/news/>
<http://www.unglobalpulse.org/about-new>

Index

Big Data

Index

ADVERTISING
A Very Short Introduction
Winston Fletcher

The book contains a short history of advertising and an explanation of how the industry works, and how each of the parties (the advertisers , the media and the agencies) are involved. It considers the extensive spectrum of advertisers and their individual needs. It also looks at the financial side of advertising and asks how advertisers know if they have been successful, or whether the money they have spent has in fact been wasted. Fletcher concludes with a discussion about the controversial and unacceptable areas of advertising such as advertising products to children and advertising products such as cigarettes and alcohol. He also discusses the benefits of advertising and what the future may hold for the industry.

www.oup.com/vsi

CANCER
A Very Short Introduction
Nick James

Cancer research is a major economic activity. There are constant improvements in treatment techniques that result in better cure rates and increased quality and quantity of life for those with the disease, yet stories of breakthroughs in a cure for cancer are often in the media. In this *Very Short Introduction* Nick James, founder of the CancerHelp UK website, examines the trends in diagnosis and treatment of the disease, as well as its economic consequences. Asking what cancer is and what causes it, he considers issues surrounding expensive drug development, what can be done to reduce the risk of developing cancer, and the use of complementary and alternative therapies.

www.oup.com/vsi

Economics
A Very Short Introduction
Partha Dasgupta

Economics has the capacity to offer us deep insights into some of the most formidable problems of life, and offer solutions to them too. Combining a global approach with examples from everyday life, Partha Dasgupta describes the lives of two children who live very different lives in different parts of the world: in the Mid-West USA and in Ethiopia. He compares the obstacles facing them, and the processes that shape their lives, their families, and their futures. He shows how economics uncovers these processes, finds explanations for them, and how it forms policies and solutions.

> 'An excellent introduction . . . presents mathematical and statistical findings in straightforward prose.'
>
> Financial Times

FREE SPEECH
A Very Short Introduction
Nigel Warburton

'I disapprove of what you say, but I will defend to the death your right to say it' This slogan, attributed to Voltaire, is frequently quoted by defenders of free speech. Yet it is rare to find anyone prepared to defend all expression in every circumstance, especially if the views expressed incite violence. So where do the limits lie? What is the real value of free speech? Here, Nigel Warburton offers a concise guide to important questions facing modern society about the value and limits of free speech: Where should a civilized society draw the line? Should we be free to offend other people's religion? Are there good grounds for censoring pornography? Has the Internet changed everything? This Very Short Introduction is a thought-provoking, accessible, and up-to-date examination of the liberal assumption that free speech is worth preserving at any cost.

'The genius of Nigel Warburton's *Free Speech* lies not only in its extraordinary clarity and incisiveness. Just as important is the way Warburton addresses freedom of speech - and attempts to stifle it - as an issue for the 21st century. More than ever, we need this book.'

Denis Dutton, University of Canterbury, New Zealand

GLOBALIZATION
A Very Short Introduction
Manfred Steger

'Globalization' has become one of the defining buzzwords
of our time - a term that describes a variety of accelerating
economic, political, cultural, ideological, and environmental
processes that are rapidly altering our experience of the world.
It is by its nature a dynamic topic - and this *Very Short
Introduction* has been fully updated for 2009, to include
developments in global politics, the impact of terrorism, and
environmental issues. Presenting globalization in accessible
language as a multifaceted process encompassing global,
regional, and local aspects of social life, Manfred B. Steger
looks at its causes and effects, examines whether it is a new
phenomenon, and explores the question of whether,
ultimately, globalization is a good or a bad thing.

www.oup.com/vsi